Analysing Teaching–Learning Interactions
in Higher Education

Also available from Continuum

Changing Pedagogy, Xin-min Zheng and Chris Davison

The Consumer Experience of Higher Education, Deirdre McArdle-Clinton

Lifelong Learning, Jim Smith and Andrea Spurling

Pedagogy and the University, Monica McLean

Perspectives of Quality in Adult Learning, Peter Boshier

Teaching and Learning in Higher Education, Harriet Evans

Widening Participation in Post-Compulsory Education, Liz Thomas

Analysing Teaching–Learning Interactions in Higher Education

Accounting for Structure and Agency

PAUL ASHWIN

continuum

Continuum
The Tower Building, 11 York Road, London SE1 7NX
80 Maiden Lane, Suite 704, New York NY 10038

www.continuumbooks.com

British Library Cataloguing-in-Publication Data
A catalogue record for this book is available from the British Library.

ISBN: 978-0-8264-9418-4 (hardcover)

Library of Congress Cataloging-in-Publication Data
Ashwin, Paul, 1970–
    Analysing teaching–learning interactions in higher education : accounting for
structure and agency / Paul Ashwin.
        p. cm.
    Includes bibliographical references.
    ISBN 978-0-8264-9418-4 (hardback)
    1. College teaching. 2. Teacher-student relationships. 3. Interaction analysis in
education. I. Title.

378.1'25–dc22

2008046617

Typeset by Kenneth Burnley, Wirral, Cheshire
Printed and bound in Great Britain by . . .

Contents

To my wonderful Emma

Acknowledgements

Many people have contributed to the development and writing of this book. There are a few whom I wish to thank particularly. Carolyn Jackson, Monica McLean, Keith Trigwell, Murray Saunders and Paul Trowler all spent time discussing different aspects of the ideas that I explore in this book and assisted considerably in their development. I have been fortunate to be a member of the Department of Educational Research, Lancaster University, in which students and staff alike are willing to discuss the difficult issues around how to generate and make sense of data about teaching and learning. In particular, the discussions I have had with students on the Doctoral Programme in Educational Research and the MA in Education/Educational Research contributed greatly to my understanding of the issues I explore, as did my discussions with members of the Teaching and Learning Cultures Reading Group. I'd also like to thank my department and Lancaster University for the term of sabbatical leave that gave me the space in which to begin developing the arguments in this book.

Finally, I'd like to thank my family for their encouragement and care; especially Emma and Rosa who have had to put up with my preoccupied moodiness as I have completed this book.

PAUL ASHWIN

Chapter 1

Introduction

As its title suggests, this is a book about analysing teaching–learning interactions in higher education. It asks questions such as: when an academic engages with a group of students in a seminar, how is the interaction affected by the actions and reactions of those involved? What impact does the teaching–learning environment have on this ongoing interaction? How do the identities of students and academics influence the ways in which they respond to each other? Does the disciplinary focus of the material that students and academics discuss influence the ways in which they engage together? Does the particular institution in which this interaction takes place have an impact on the developing form of the interaction? In addressing such questions, I discuss ways of accounting for social structure and individual agency in analysing teaching–learning interactions in higher education.

There are three broad aspects to the argument that I develop in this book. First, I offer a critique of the way in which current research into teaching–learning processes in higher education analyses teaching–learning interactions and the way in which it accounts for social structure and individual agency within these interactions. Second, I explore alternative ways of analysing teaching–learning interactions that give a sense of their dynamic nature and the way in which they relate to wider social processes. Third, I examine the implications for future research of both my critique of current, and my consideration of alternative, approaches to analysing teaching–learning interactions in higher education.

In order to provide an initial sense of this argument, in this chapter I address the question of why any of this matters. After an initial word about terminology, I tackle the issue of why teaching–learning interactions in higher education matter and what are the problems with the current mainstream approaches to analysing these interactions. A danger of focusing on teaching–learning interactions is that a sense

1

can be lost of how particular interactions are shaped by processes that stretch far beyond them. In order to avoid this, I consider issues relating to how to account for both the structured and agentic aspects of teaching–learning interactions. I then provide an outline of the structure and argument of the rest of the book, before considering the limits of my argument.

An initial word about terminology

As will be clear from the title and first few paragraphs of this book, I have chosen to use the perhaps clumsy terminology of 'teaching–learning' interactions and 'teaching–learning' processes. While this will not be the only awkward terminology adopted in this book (see Chapter 2 for the argument for the use of the phrase 'structural–agentic processes'), I want to explain the use of this particular terminology from the outset. This is because it provides a sense of some of the issues that are central to this book.

I use the term 'teaching–learning' rather than the more common 'teaching and learning' or 'learning and teaching' because I want to move away from the idea that teaching and learning are two discrete and separable processes. Instead I want to emphasize that they are different aspects of the same processes in which students and academics engage together. This is clearly related to my focus on teaching–learning interactions but I use this terminology for two other reasons.

First, I wish to move away from the tacit assumption that 'teaching' is embodied in a 'teacher' and 'learning' is embodied in a 'learner'. The move away from this assumption is related to challenging the idea that the 'teacher just teaches' and the 'learner just learns' in teaching–learning interactions and the related separation of academics' role as 'teachers' and students' role as 'learners' from other aspects of their lives within and beyond higher education. For this reason, in this book I mainly use the terminology of 'academic' and 'student' to talk about those who engage in teaching–learning interactions.

Second, I wish to avoid debates of whether it should be 'learning and teaching' or 'teaching and learning' (see Edwards 2006 for a fascinating discussion of the 'and'). While this section indicates my belief that how things are talked about helps to shape the way in which they are experienced, the question of which order two parts of a single set of processes should be placed in, seems to me to be largely factious.

In writing about teaching–learning interactions, I am particularly focused on interactions that are intended to support students in engaging with the curricula of their higher education programmes. Thus while I write mainly in terms of academics and students, it is clear that other people may be involved in such interactions. Equally, I am not simply focusing on face-to-face interactions. Clearly students and academics can interact at a distance. While this can happen via teaching–learning technologies, I have more than this is mind. When a student reads feedback on an assignment, this for me can be described as a teaching–learning interaction. Thus within this book teaching–learning interactions are situations in which students engage with other students, academics or support staff in relation to the curricula of their programmes, even if they are separated by location or time.

Beyond this rough and ready definition, the question of distinguishing between teaching–learning interactions and other types of interactions is not something that particularly concerns me in this book. This is not because this is an unimportant issue but rather, as I argue in Chapter 2, it is because it is those who analyse interactions who characterize them as particular kinds of interactions rather than different kinds of interactions existing 'out there' waiting to be recognized.

I use the term 'teaching–learning processes' as a more generic way of describing the processes related to teaching and learning in higher education. Thus teaching–learning processes include teaching–learning interactions but they also include non-interactive aspects of such processes, such as the practices of academics-as-teachers as distinct from the practices of students-as-learners. The reason for this distinction is that a central part of my argument is that while research in higher education has focused on teaching–learning processes, it has not focused on teaching–learning interactions.

There are two further points that I need to emphasize. First, I do not distinguish between teaching–learning processes and assessment processes in higher education. I take the view that assessment processes are an essential part of teaching–learning processes. Second, I do not distinguish between different levels of higher education. While much of the literature that I refer to is drawn from undergraduate higher education, I see my arguments as equally relevant to both taught and research-based postgraduate higher education. The forms and focus of the teaching–learning interactions may vary but the relations between such interactions and wider social processes can be addressed in similar ways to those which I discuss in this book.

Why focus on teaching–learning interactions in higher education?

In answering the question of why teaching–learning interactions in higher education matter, it is tempting to ask another question. If they do not matter, why do universities spend a great deal of their resources on setting up situations in which students are supposed to learn through interacting with academics, support staff and other students? Something is supposed to happen in these situations in which these groups come together that is of value in helping students to engage with the programmes they are studying and helping academics and support staff to understand the needs of their students.

In texts aimed at improving teaching–learning processes in higher education, the dynamic nature of these interactions is seen to be crucial in promoting high-quality student learning. Thus Ramsden (2003, pp. 98–9) argues that all the principles of good teaching can be derived from the idea that 'good teaching is open to change; it involves constantly trying to find out what the effects of instruction are on learning, and modifying that instruction in the light of the evidence collected'. Similarly Prosser and Trigwell (1999) emphasize the con-textual dependency of teaching–learning interactions, highlighting that they can play out in very different ways depending on the situation in which the interaction is taking place. Finally, McKeachie (1974, p. 11) elegantly summarizes the importance of the dynamic nature of teaching–learning interactions:

> Fortunately most educational situations are interactive situations in which a developing, learning human being engages with a situation in ways designed to meet [her or] his learning needs. Part of that situation is another human being who has some resources for instruction and some capacity to adapt to the learner. It is this that makes education both endlessly challenging and deeply humane.

While the importance of the dynamic nature of teaching–learning interactions is clearly recognized in texts aimed at improving teaching–learning processes in higher education, the interactive aspects of such processes are currently put in the background of research in this area. There are two mainstream approaches to analysing teaching–learning processes in higher education: the 'Approaches to Learning and Teaching' perspective and 'Social Practice' perspectives (in Chapter 4 I will split this into a number of different perspectives). It is important to be clear that both of these perspectives have made significant contributions to the understanding of teaching–learning processes within higher education. The Approaches to Learning and Teaching research (for excellent summaries see Prosser and Trigwell 1999; Richardson 2005; Entwistle 2007) has given a clear indication of how students' and academics' perceptions of teaching–learning environments are consistently related to the quality of their learning and teaching and to the quality of students' learning outcomes. Research from a Social Practice perspective has provided insights into the issues that students face in understanding the cultural context of their programmes of study (for example, see Lea and Street 1998; Jones *et al.* 1999; Mann 2000; Lillis 2001) and the impact that institutional and disciplinary settings have on academics' understanding of their teaching (for example, see Trowler and Cooper 2002).

However, these perspectives are less helpful for analysing the dynamic nature of teaching–learning interactions in higher education. As I discuss in more detail in Chapter 3, the focus within the Approaches to Learning and Teaching perspective tends to be on either students' or academics' *perceptions* of teaching–learning processes in higher education. Thus this research views these processes from the perspective of either academics or students, which means there is little sense of the ongoing, dynamic interplay between academics and students within particular teaching–learning interactions.

Within Social Practice perspectives on researching teaching–learning processes in higher education, research tends to focus on learning practices or the practice of students (for example, see Lea and Street 1998; Mann 2000; Lillis 2001) or teaching practices or the practice of teachers (for example, see Trowler and Cooper 2002). This approach is problematic in relation to analysing the dynamic nature of teaching–learning interactions for two reasons. First, as I argue in

Chapter 3, when foregrounding social practices it becomes clear that academics and students are engaged in different types of practices. Second, social practices are seen to be fairly durable ways of approaching particular tasks that are largely taken for granted by those who engage in them (for example, see Trowler 2005). Thus the focus tends to be on the *stability* of practices rather than the distinctive ways in which they play out in particular teaching–learning interactions.

It is important to be clear that I am arguing that this is a tendency, rather than an inevitable consequence, of adopting these ways of analysing teaching–learning processes in higher education. As I have already indicated, there is some recognition of the dynamic and interactive aspects of these processes. However, my argument is that in using the language of 'perceptions' and 'practices', the dynamic and shifting aspects of teaching–learning interactions tend to be obscured. In this book, I examine ways of analysing teaching–learning processes that foreground these dynamic and shifting elements, not because they are the only important aspects of such processes but because they are important elements that are currently under-explored in research in higher education.

Why focus on accounting for structure and agency in teaching–learning interactions in higher education?

A crucial issue that is raised by analysing the dynamic aspects of teaching–learning interactions is that this can be taken to imply that everything that matters within such an analysis is contained within the interaction itself. Thus the explanation of what happened in a particular teaching–learning interaction is taken to be located within what occurred between those involved in the interaction. My argument in this book is that such a move would be a mistake. This is because in order to understand what happened within a particular teaching–learning interaction it is necessary to understand how the interaction was shaped by processes that might not be visible within the interaction.

The issues I am raising here are issues about what counts as an explanation within research into teaching–learning interactions in higher education. I am arguing that in order to understand such interactions it is necessary to develop both a sense of how these reflect the intentions and practices of students and academics and how they are shaped by wider social processes. In doing so, I am raising questions of how to account for structure and agency in research into teaching–learning interactions in higher education. As I have argued before (see Ashwin 2008), while such issues are routinely discussed in debates around social theory generally (for example Bourdieu 1977; 1990a; Giddens 1984; Archer 1995; Mouzelis 1995; Layder 1997; Byrne 1998; Flyvbjerg 2001; Sibeon 2004), in research into teaching–learning processes in higher education these issues are hardly discussed at all (although for exceptions see Trowler 1998; Fanghanel 2004, 2006; Shay 2005; McLean 2006).

These issues matter because there is strong evidence that the higher education systems are shaped by the societies in which they operate. To take the UK as an example, while access to undergraduate higher education has slowly widened over recent years (see Gorard 2005, 2008), there is a clear pattern of more privileged students, for example in terms of social class, attending more prestigious universities (Ashworth 2004; Brennan and Osborne 2008; Crozier *et al.* 2008). This is increasingly important as the field of higher education becomes more diversified, with different institutions offering different kinds of higher education (Brennan and Naidoo 2008; Teichler 2008). The interpretation of such patterns needs to be handled carefully. For example, as Gorard (2005, 2008) and Gorard *et al.* (2007) argue, there is no evidence of systematic bias during the admissions process on the part of universities. Rather than the outcome of simple prejudice or deliberate unfairness, such patterns appear to be the result of the coming together of many complex social processes including the impact of early childhood experiences and education (Forsyth and Furlong 2003; Gorard *et al.* 2007), differences in the familial familiarity with higher education (Thomas and Quinn 2007), differences in the ways in which students choose their degree programmes (Hutchings 2003a; Reay *et al.* 2001, 2005; Gorard *et al.* 2007), as well as differences in the relative cost of (Hutchings 2003b), and relative value assigned to (Archer 2003), higher education.

There is evidence, albeit more limited, of similar complex social processes impacting on students' experience of higher education in different countries (Archer and Leathwood 2003; Forsyth and Furlong 2003; Read *et al.* 2003; Ostrove and Long 2007; Brennan and Osborne

2008; Crozier *et al.* 2008) and their outcomes in terms of achievement (Quinn 2004; Helland 2007; Richardson 2008; Severiens and Wolff 2008; Tumen *et al.* 2008) and progression to further study and employment (Furlong and Cartmel 2005; Brooks 2006; Brooks and Everett 2008a; Brennan and Naidoo 2008).

While such patterns appear to be the unintended consequences of complex social processes, the effects that they indicate are still real. Given the way in which such processes appear to structure entry to, experiences of, and outcomes from engagement in higher education, it seems extremely likely that they will play a role in shaping teaching–learning processes in higher education. Therefore, it is perhaps surprising that until recently the impact of social structures on teaching–learning processes in higher education has not been a central concern of research in this area. Although this situation is changing (see Brennan and Osborne 2008; Crozier *et al.* 2008 for two recent projects that have highlighted this issue), part of my argument is that this is because the mainstream approaches to analysing teaching–learning processes in higher education tend not to foreground such questions. This is both a conceptual and a methodological problem.

For the Approaches to Learning and Teaching perspective it is largely a conceptual problem. As I argued earlier, this perspective is focused on students' and academics' *perceptions* of teaching–learning environments in higher education. This means that it highlights students' and academics' intentions within teaching–learning processes rather than the way in which these intentions are shaped by other social processes. This means that as a perspective it is firmly rooted in considerations of agency. Anything that operates outside of these perceptions is bracketed outside of explanations offered. This is reminiscent of Apple's (1979) criticism of phenomenology that it 'inclines us to forget that there *are* objective institutions and structures "out there" that have power, that control our lives and our very perception' (p. 140).

While the conceptual approach of Social Practice perspectives highlights the ways in which perceptions are structured, research projects from these perspectives often come up against a methodological problem. This is because many studies from these perspectives are based upon students' and academics' accounts of teaching–learning processes, whether generated by interviews or questionnaires. This means that such research is still largely based on students' and academics' perceptions of teaching–learning processes and it is again difficult to get a sense of how their accounts might be shaped by wider social processes.

It is not that these perspectives do not give a sense of what structures teaching–learning processes in higher education. As I argue in Chapter 3, there is actually quite a lot of discussion of the factors that structure these processes. It is rather that because they are based on the accounts of students and academics, these structuring factors are only explored from the perspectives of students and academics. My argument is that this gives a fairly two-dimensional view of these factors rather than a detailed sense of the relations between these factors and teaching–learning processes.

Outline of the structure and argument of this book

In this book I examine alternative perspectives that can analyse the relations between teaching–learning interactions in higher education and the factors that shape them. It is clear that the way in which structure and agency are conceived will be crucial in informing the approaches that are taken to examining these relations. Beyond research into higher education, educational research in general does not have a particularly illustrious history of tackling issues of structure and agency. Hammersley (1986) and Gewirtz and Cribb (2003) outline many of the difficulties that have faced those trying to engage with these difficult issues. In Chapter 2, I develop an argument for how I will approach issues of structure and agency. I situate this argument within a view of the social world as incredibly complex, which can only be understood by using concepts that simplify its complexity. I argue that an implication of this view is that difficulties relating to structure and agency are difficulties related to understanding and developing knowledge about the social world rather than a problem relating to the nature of the social world itself. Thus rather than, for example, structure and agency representing two different types of substances within the social world (social structures and individual actors), I argue that they represent two different ways of characterizing sets of social processes – one that foregrounds the ways in which individual actors shape the world and the other that foregrounds the ways in which the world shapes individual actors. Based on this, I argue that in examining sets of complex processes that shape teaching–learning interactions there is a need to characterize both their structural and their agentic aspects. Thus I refer to these processes as 'structural–agentic' processes. In doing so, I argue that it is necessary to explain both how such processes are situated in teaching–learning interactions and how teaching–learning interactions can be described in terms of structural–agentic processes.

In Chapter 3, I argue that research into teaching–learning processes has consistently identified four sets of structural–agentic processes that are important in teaching–learning interactions in higher education. These are the teaching–learning environment; the identities of students and academics; the disciplinary knowledge practices that are the focus of the interaction; and the cultures of the institution in which the teaching–learning interaction is situated. I use the argument I developed in Chapter 2 to critically examine the current mainstream perspectives in research into teaching–learning processes that are available for analysing the relations between these structural–agentic processes and teaching–learning interactions in higher education. Given that these perspectives were not developed with this purpose in mind, it is perhaps not surprising that I argue that they are not particularly suited for analysing these relations.

In Chapters 4 to 7, I draw on a different perspective to analyse the relations between each set of structural–agentic processes and teaching–learning interactions in higher education. While each of these perspectives has been used to inform some research into teaching–learning processes in higher education, they are less established within this research than the perspectives I examined in Chapter 3. In Chapter 4, I examine the relations between teaching–learning environments and teaching–learning interactions from an Activity Theory perspective. In Chapter 5, I examine the relations between the identities of students and academics and teaching–learning interactions from the perspective of Symbolic Interactionism. In Chapter 6, I examine the relations between disciplinary knowledge practices and teaching–learning interactions from a Bernsteinian perspective, and, in Chapter 7, I examine the relations between institutional cultures and teaching–learning interactions from a Bourdieusian perspective.

In each case, I argue that the alternative perspective offers new insight into analysing the relations between structural–agentic processes and teaching–learning interactions that are not offered by the perspectives examined in Chapter 3. In particular, I argue that they each provide a framework for understanding how the respective sets of structural–agentic processes are situated in teaching–learning interactions and how teaching–learning interactions can be characterized in terms of the structural–agentic processes. This means that over the course of the four chapters I examine four different ways in which sets of structural–agentic processes become situated in teaching–learning interactions, and four different ways of characterizing teaching–learning interactions in higher education.

It is important to be clear that, because the different perspectives on teaching–learning interactions simplify them in different ways, they are not independent of each other. Rather, they overlap with each other in a number of different and differing ways. This has two implications. First, in examining the relations between each set of structural–agentic processes and teaching–learning interactions in higher education, I suggest how research from other perspectives can be interpreted in ways that are congruent with the perspective under discussion. Due to the overlaps in the perspectives, I sometimes draw on the same evidence to inform different chapters. This means that this evidence is doing slightly different work each time it is used because it is being interpreted from a different perspective. It also means that this involves a reinterpretation of this research rather than a claim that this is what is argued for within the original research. I return to this issue in the conclusion of this chapter. Second, these overlaps between the perspectives examined suggest two ways in which Chapters 3 to 7 can be read. Either they can be read in the order presented, or those interested in particular sets of structural–agentic processes can move straight from the relevant section in Chapter 3 to the chapter examining the corresponding set of structural–agentic processes.

In Chapter 8, I examine the conceptual and methodological implications of my arguments in Chapters 2 to 7 for analysing teaching–learning interactions in higher education. I argue that while the range of perspectives I have examined is not intended to be exhaustive, it is possible to suggest that some ways of analysing teaching–learning interactions are 'more helpful' than others in attempting to understand the relations between such interactions and sets of structural–agentic processes. To support this, I develop an argument for evaluating what might count as a 'more helpful' perspective. I then examine the methodological implications of my argument, in terms of what it means for the ways in which data relating to teaching–learning inter-actions are generated and analysed. I bring these two sets of implica-tions together by considering what they mean for future research into teaching–learning interactions in higher education. In doing so I again emphasize the complex and messy nature of teaching–learning interactions and the difficulties that face researchers who wish to develop knowledge about them.

The limits of my arguments

In concluding this introductory chapter, I want to be clear that the arguments that I develop in this book are related to my interests in, and experiences of, researching teaching–learning processes in higher and further education (for example, see Ashwin 2003a,b, 2005, 2006a,b). They grew out of my concerns about how to conceptualize and generate knowledge about the dynamic and shifting aspects of teaching–learning interactions while also understanding how such interactions were structured by wider social processes. It is important to be clear about this because the arguments I develop are related to undertaking this particular task. There are two implications of this that I want to emphasize.

First, it means that my criticisms of the current research into teaching–learning processes in higher education are criticisms of it in relation to the task of understanding the relations between sets of structural–agentic processes and teaching–learning interactions. As I have already indicated, the vast majority of this research was never intended to help with this task. I want to emphasize this now, and also do so in later chapters, because I think that too much criticism of different perspectives on researching teaching–learning processes in higher education involves criticizing research for not doing things that it was never intended to do. In looking at ways of analysing the relations between sets of structural–agentic processes and teaching–learning interactions in higher education, I clearly need to show why current approaches are not suitable. However, this should not be taken as implying that I think these research perspectives are not helpful for asking other kinds of questions about teaching–learning processes in higher education.

Second, in relation to the alternative perspectives I examine in Chapters 4 to 7, it means that I came to each of the perspectives with a focus on teaching–learning interactions in higher education rather than a thorough grounding in their more sociological concerns. Thus in applying the perspectives to analysing the relations between particular sets of structural–agentic processes and teaching–learning interactions, I am engaged in what Bernstein (1990, 2000) would call the 'recontextualizing' of these ideas. This means that in applying these ideas to this particular set of problems, I have a particular take on them and am using them in particular ways. This means that I am not claiming to offer pure accounts of Activity Theory, Symbolic Interactionism, Bernstein or Bourdieu but am rather showing aspects of these approaches that might be helpful in understanding the relations between particular sets of structural–agentic processes and teaching–learning interactions.

Emphasizing these limits of my arguments is not intended to absolve me from any misunderstandings of the perspectives that I discuss. Rather, it is intended to highlight that in developing a deep understanding of the complexity of teaching–learning processes in higher education, it is necessary to have different ways of understanding different aspects of such processes. It is to a further discussion of this issue that I turn in the next chapter.

Chapter 2

Conceptualizing structure and agency in relation to teaching–learning interactions

Introduction

In the previous chapter, I argued that current approaches to researching teaching–learning processes in higher education have two significant and related shortcomings when it comes to analysing teaching–learning interactions. First, they do not highlight the dynamic and interactive aspects of teaching–learning processes, and second, they do not highlight issues of accounting for structure and agency in such research.

In this chapter, I develop an argument for the conceptualization of structure and agency that will inform the remaining chapters of this book. To underpin this conceptualization of structure and agency, I first briefly discuss the approach that I take to understanding the nature of the social world (ontology) and the nature of knowledge about the social world (epistemology). I then outline the conceptualization of structure and agency before examining the implications of this conceptualization for analysing teaching–learning interactions in higher education.

It is important to emphasize that my examination of issues of structure and agency is informed by my focus on teaching–learning interactions in higher education. This has two implications. First, it means that my interest is in developing a conception of structure and agency that can help in understanding the dynamic aspects of teaching–learning interactions. This purpose will inevitably shape the conception of structure and agency that is developed. Second, it is important to be clear that in this chapter, while I draw upon social theory to make my argument for a particular approach to conceptualizing structure and agency, there is no claim that my arguments are innovative in relation to social theory. In Mouzelis's (1995, pp. 3–4) terms, I am using social theory as a 'tool' 'for looking at social phenomena in such a way that interesting questions are generated and methodologically proper linkages established between levels of analysis' rather than arguing that my account of structure and agency is, in itself, an 'end-product'.

Ontology and epistemology

Before examining how I conceptualize structure and agency, I first examine the view of the social world (ontology) and knowledge of the social world (epistemology) that underpins this conceptualization. The views taken of ontology and epistemology are clearly central to developing a sense of how to generate knowledge of the social world (methodology). This is important because many of the implications for researching teaching–learning interactions in higher education raised by a consideration of structure and agency are methodological (see Chapter 8 and Ashwin 2008).

Ontology

The view taken of the social world in the conception of structure and agency that is outlined below is 'realist' (see Sayer 1992, 2000). Within this view the social world is seen as *real* in that it exists independently of our knowledge of it (Sayer 1992). The social world is *complex* in that it is made up of a large number of elements, is uncertain and unpredictable, and is *emergent* (Sayer 1992, 2000; Sibeon 2004). Sayer (2000, p. 12) defines emergence as: 'situations in which the conjunction of two or more features or aspects give rise to new phenomena, which have properties which are irreducible to those of their constituents, even though the latter are necessary for their existence'. As Sayer (1992, 2000) indicates, the standard example of emergence within the physical world is water, which is made up of hydrogen and oxygen but has emergent properties that are different from those of either of these constituent parts.

Before moving on to examine epistemology, it is worth pointing out that while the position I adopt is 'realist', it is not a 'critical realist' position (Sayer 1992, 2000; Archer 1995, 2003). As will become clear below, while I draw on critical realist ideas, there are differences between my position and critical realism. Equally, while within the view outlined above the world is seen as complex, this does not entail a commitment to 'complexity theory' (see Byrne 1998 and in an educational context Morrison 2002; Haggis 2006).

Epistemology

So if the social world is real and complex, what of our knowledge of it? The position adopted here is that it is not possible to have direct and unmediated access to the social world and therefore it cannot be known directly. Rather, the world can only be known through our constructs of it. For analysing teaching–learning interactions in higher education, this means that such interactions have to be approached with some conception or theory of what is going on. These theories are inevitably simplifications, in that they cannot deal with the complexity of the social world but instead focus on certain aspects and not others. This means that, as Law (2004) argues, events and processes exceed our capacity to know them.

This view of epistemology has a number of implications. First as Sayer (1992, p. 232) argues, this means that knowledge of the world is fallible and theory laden and 'explanations are relatively incomplete, approximate and contestable'. Second, it suggests that no one theory can encompass all aspects of the social world and thus different theories will focus on different aspects of the social world (Hammersley 1986). These differences in focus mean that different ways of understanding a social situation may not be compatible. This means that it is not possible to synthesize all theories together and attempts at such synthesis will lead to oversimplifications of the social world (Hammersley 1986; Mol and Law 2002). Rather, as Mol and Law (2002, p. 11) argue, 'It becomes instead a matter of determining which simplification or simplifications we will attend to and create and, as we do this, of attending to what they foreground and draw attention to, as well as what they relegate to the background.' However, as Strathern (2002) argues, it is possible to shift between these different simplifications in order to examine what understanding of the social world is offered by their different foci.

This does not mean that researchers are free to construct the world in any way they choose, for two reasons. First, the theories through which the world is simplified are produced socially rather than individually. Thus the perspectives that researchers draw on to simplify the world are developed collectively and even new perspectives are dependent on existing ways of seeing the world. This means that individual researchers cannot just generate new ways of simplifying the world but do so in the context of existing simplifications. Second, if they are to develop a deeper understanding of the social world, then researchers need to develop theories and constructs that have the space in which to be challenged and developed by its messy reality. This point has important implications for the theories that are used to analyse teaching–learning interactions in higher education, and is examined in more detail in Chapter 8.

Conceptualizing structure and agency

There are two implications of this view of ontology and epistemology for an approach to understanding structure and agency. First, this view suggests that the 'structure and agency problem' is a product of the ways in which theory *has* to be used in order to interpret the empirical world rather than a feature of social world. This means that rather than being an ontological question, related to the nature of the social world as is often claimed in social theory (for example, see Giddens 1984; Archer 1995, 2003; Layder 1997; Sibeon 2004), it is an epistemological question, related to how to develop explanations of the social world. In other words, the issues of structure and agency are not issues of whether there are different types of properties in the social world (those relating to structure and those relating to agency) but rather they are issues of how different types of conceptualizations are used to develop different kinds of explanations of a complex social world.

Second, because the social world is conceived of as dynamic and emergent, both the structural and agentic aspects of such phenomena are seen as processes rather than 'things'. So although there is a tendency to talk of 'social structure' or 'individual agency' as if they are objects, the view of structure and agency that I am arguing for examines them as processes. I think there are two reasons for the tendency to treat these processes as things. One is related to the position that one adopts: so that when one is examining the projects of individual agents, structural processes take on the *appearance* of structures; social class or race becomes a 'thing' rather than a dynamic process or from the perspective of a structural approach, individuals *appear* to be mere 'place holders' rather than dynamic individuals. Both of these are due to the simplifying effects of the perspective from which the analysis is being undertaken rather than a feature of the world 'out there'. The other reason is related to power. Law (1994) characterizes this tendency in terms of 'verbs' trying to become 'nouns' and argues that if you can convert a verb into a noun, then you achieve greater durability and thus there is an interest in translating a 'process' into a 'thing'.

This means that when I ask the question, 'How can we account for structure and agency in teaching–learning interactions?', the question I am asking is actually about how to view teaching-interactions in a way that can explain these complex social processes in both agentic and structural terms. In this way I am arguing that structure and agency are not different *kinds* of processes but different ways of grouping or conceptualizing complex social processes. Thus they can represent the *same* processes viewed through a different lens or *under a different description* (Davidson 1980). To take as an example the differences in the social class composition of students at different universities, which I discussed in Chapter 1: these can be viewed agentically in terms of university applicants' active choice processes or they can be viewed structurally in terms of the differential ways in which social class shapes the educational expectations and qualifications of applicants. The point is that these are not different processes but are different ways of describing broadly the same social processes. This means that different descriptions of these processes will position their agentic and structural aspects in different ways. For this reason, I use the perhaps rather ugly term 'structural–agentic processes' to indicate that the same processes can be described in both structural and agentic terms.

'Structural–agentic' descriptions of social processes

So what makes a description of a set of complex processes 'structural' or 'agentic'? The approach that I take to this is to develop 'minimal' concepts of each of these terms (see Hindess 1988, 1989; Sibeon 2004). I do this to allow the maximum amount of space for the complex and emergent social world while still developing a clear sense of the differences between the two terms.

The minimal concept of describing the agentic and structural aspects of social processes that will be adopted in this book is based on the work of Margaret Archer (1995, 2003). This sees agency in terms of the projects of human agents, and structure in terms of the factors that enable or constrain such projects. It is important to be clear that while Archer (2003, p. 2) sees structure and agency as 'distinct strata of reality', my argument is that these are different ways of characterizing social processes. Thus, I am drawing on Archer's (1995, 2003) approach to differentiating structure and agency but am arguing that it should be seen as an epistemological rather than an ontological distinction.

As I summarized above, an agentic description of set a processes is one which examines the ways in which these processes are shaped by the intentions and projects of agents. It should be noted that this conception of agentic descriptions of processes does not limit them to individuals. For example, the conception and acting on of projects by groups are seen as agentic processes, even though they cannot be reduced to the agency of any single individual in situations where decisions emerge in the course of discussions (Hindess 1989). This aspect of the agentic view of social processes is important if teaching–learning processes in higher education are not to be reduced to individual activities. For example, research into distributed cognition (for example, see Salomon 1993) suggests that there are many situations in which knowledge is the intentional product of collective, rather than individual, enterprises.

Structural descriptions of sets of social processes are focused on examining the factors that enable and constrain the projects of agents. While the idea that agents are capable of making and acting on projects means that they have some awareness of what they are doing and why, this does not mean that they are always fully aware of the factors that enable or constrain their projects, or of all of the potential outcomes of their projects. As Sayer (2000, p. 20) argues, 'Much of what happens does not depend on or correspond to agents' understandings; there are unintended consequences and unacknowledged conditions and things can happen to people regardless of their understandings.' This conception of structural processes moves away from describing social structures in terms of recurring patterns in social organization (see López and Scott 2000 for a discussion of this approach to social structure) and instead seeks to understand how social processes shape the collective or individual projects of agents (Archer 1995, 2003).

Following from the previous definitions, structural–agentic descriptions of social processes attempt to give a sense of both the intentional projects of individual and collective agents, and the ways in which these projects are enabled and constrained. So in examining teaching–learning interactions in higher education, this involves finding ways of conceptualizing these interactions that can offer both of these kinds of description. As I argued in my discussion of epistemology, different ways of conceptualizing teaching–learning interactions will characterize them as different kinds of social processes. For this reason, I argue that different perspectives are required in order to analyse the relations between different sets of structural–agentic processes and teaching–learning interactions.

At this stage it is important to emphasize once again that it is the researchers or analysts who group different processes under the descriptions of 'teaching–learning interactions' and different 'structural–agentic processes'. However, as I argued earlier, this does not mean that any processes can be grouped under any description. Instead, empirical data need to be used to question any grouping and labelling of processes. In this way, as Law (1994) argues, researchers need to be modest and tentative and always question how much of their categorizations reflect the empirical world and how much they reflect their conceptualizations. This ongoing tentative construction and questioning is one reason why research is always, to some extent, unfinished and incomplete.

Other questions: of power and the relation to the micro/macro debate

There are two questions about this approach to structure and agency that I would now like to address. The first is the question of where is power in the account of structural–agentic processes, and the second is the question of how this conception of structural–agentic processes relates to the debates around the difference between micro and macro social phenomena.

First, the question of how power is seen in this account of structural–agentic processes. My response to this is that questions about such processes are questions about power. They are about how much *power* the projects of students and academics have to shape teaching–learning interactions in higher education and how much *power* structural–agentic processes have in shaping these interactions. Thus power is everywhere within this conception of structure and agency. However, it is described differently under agentic and structural descriptions of such processes. Under agentic descriptions it is *relational*, that is it plays out in different ways in different situations, while in structural descriptions it is *systemic*, it is related to how agents are positioned (see Sibeon 2004 for a discussion of these two views of power). Again, both ways of describing power need to be accounted for. Thus while academics in a particular teaching–learning interaction might have more systemic power than students, different academics will use this power in different ways and it will play out differently depending on students' reactions to this power.

Second, how does this view of structural–agentic processes relate to the 'macro/micro' divide? From the perspective adopted here, there is a rejection of the conflation of agency with micro contexts and structure with macro contexts (see Sibeon 2004 for a discussion of this). As I hope is clear, structural–agentic processes are present in both contexts, as micro–macro is about the scale of the social context considered rather than about a focus on describing the structural or agentic aspects of processes. Thus in considering teaching–learning interactions in higher education, the context is a micro one, but, as I have argued, the focus is on both the structural and agentic aspects of the processes that shape and are formed in these interactions. However, my focus on a micro context does have an impact on the way in which I have conceived structural–agentic processes, as it foregrounds the agentic descriptions of these processes more than the structural aspects. In other words, my view of structural descriptions of these processes is heavily dependent on my view of the agentic descriptions of such processes. This is because my overarching focus is on students' and academics' projects, how they impact on each other and how they are shaped by sets of structural–agentic processes in teaching–learning interactions in higher education. If my focus was, for example, on how national higher education systems are shaped by structural–agentic processes, then it seems highly likely that structural descriptions of such processes would be more in the foreground than agentic descriptions. In this way my view of structural–

agentic processes is clearly related to my interest in teaching–learning interactions in higher education.

Analysing the relations between structural–agentic processes and teaching–learning interactions in higher education

So what does this view of structure and agency mean for my examination of ways of accounting for structure and agency in teaching–learning interactions in higher education? In general it means that in analysing teaching–learning interactions, I need to examine the way in which such interactions can be described both in terms of the projects of the agents who are involved in those interactions and in terms of the ways in which these projects are shaped by other processes. This involves a focus on analysing the relations between teaching–learning interactions and other structural–agentic processes. There are four aspects to this.

First, it needs to be made clear that rather than teaching–learning interactions and other structural–agentic processes awaiting discovery in the real world, they are categorized as these kinds of processes by those researching them. This means that different ways of analysing the relations between sets of structural–agentic processes and teaching–learning interactions are not necessarily independent of each other, but instead highlight and draw together aspects of teaching–learning interactions in different ways. For example, examining the impact of disciplinary knowledge practices on teaching–learning interactions may involve some overlaps with an examination of the relations between institutional cultures and teaching–learning interactions because they are not separate processes but different ways of conceptualizing social processes. This means that bringing together analyses of different sets of structural–agentic processes is not a straightforward affair because they may examine some common, and some uncommon aspects of teaching–learning interactions. In other words, the different ways of conceiving sets of structural–agentic processes foreground and background different aspects of the teaching–learning interaction.

Second, it suggests that the processes that are seen to make up particular sets of structural–agentic processes are an integral part of teaching–learning interactions rather than teaching–learning interactions being contained within particular structural–agentic contexts. Thus rather than seeing context as a container, context is seen as a weaving together of different strands that make up particular descriptions of a set of structural–agentic processes (see Cole 1996 for a discussion of the 'container' and 'weaving' metaphors of social context). This means that rather than, in the words of Latour (2005, p. 177), allowing the 'Wolf of Context' to gobble up the interaction by saying that it was 'shaped by its context', there is a need to develop an understanding of how particular conceptualizations of sets of structural–agentic processes can be seen as giving a shape to teaching–learning inter- actions. It should be stressed that rather than suggesting that teaching–learning interactions are a junction-point of different discrete structural–agentic processes, this view emphasizes the ways in which the different characterizations of different sets of structural– agentic processes overlap.

Third, developing a structural description of teaching–learning interactions foregrounds the way in which it is shaped by a particular set of structural–agentic processes. However, these processes do not enter into teaching–learning interactions in a pure form but are refracted, changed or mediated as they come into relation to the inter- action (see Latour 2005 for a related discussion of the differences between mediators and intermediaries). This means that the processes that are conceived as making up particular sets of structural–agentic processes take on particular forms as they enter into teaching–learning interactions and that these forms can change depending on the shape of the teaching–learning interaction. Goffman (1983, p. 11) charac- terizes this as a 'loose coupling' between interactional practices and social structures and as if there were 'a membrane selecting how various externally relevant social distinctions will be managed within the interaction'. Thus developing a structural description of teaching– learning interactions involves examining how the processes that are conceived as making up a set of structural–agentic processes become situated within teaching–learning interactions.

Fourth, agentic descriptions of teaching–learning interactions will be different when examined in relation to different sets of structural– agentic processes. This is because these sets of processes will be conceived as enabling and constraining the projects of academics and students in different ways. This means that developing agentic descriptions of teaching–learning interactions involves examining the interplay of the projects of academics and students in terms of the particular characterization of constraining and enabling forces offered by a set of structural–agentic processes. Thus developing agentic descriptions of teaching–learning interactions becomes a question of examining how the dynamic, shifting aspects of the teaching–learning interaction can be characterized in terms of the particular set of structural–agentic processes.

This means that to account for structure and agency in analysing teaching–learning interaction involves examining both how particular sets of structural–agentic processes become situated in the particular teaching–learning interaction and how the teaching–learning inter-action can be characterized in terms of the set of structural–agentic processes. As I indicated in the introduction to this chapter, I am not claiming that this argument that teaching–learning interactions need to be read in two ways is new. All of the perspectives I examine in Chapters 4 to 7 offer ways of supporting what Bourdieu and Wacquant (1992) call a 'double reading' of teaching–learning interactions. However, I am claiming that this issue has not been examined in detail in relation to teaching–learning processes in higher education (although see Shay 2005 for a double reading of assessment practices).

Due to its focus on the shifting relations between teaching–learning interactions and sets of structural–agentic processes, this view of struc-tural–agentic processes encourages a focus on the shifting configuration of these sets of processes at different times and in different spaces. This differentiates this approach from Scott's (2000) account of structure and agency in relation to educational research, where much of the focus is on the sameness of the social world. This is not to claim that there is no stability in teaching–learning interactions in higher education; rather it is simply that stability should not be assumed and when it is met should be puzzled over just as much as instability.

Summary

Given the fairly involved discussions of aspects of social theory, it may be helpful at this point if I summarize my argument in relation to analysing the relations between sets of structural–agentic processes and teaching–learning interactions in higher education:

- Teaching–learning interactions in higher education occur in a complex and unpredictable social world (from the discussion of ontology).
- In order to develop knowledge of this complex social world, researchers need, in some way, to simplify teaching–learning interactions through the theories they use to construct them. Different theories simplify teaching–learning interactions in different ways by foregrounding and backgrounding different sets of structural–agentic processes (from the discussion of epistemology).
- As theories are simplifications of a complex social world, they need to allow the space for the social world to contradict and develop them (from the discussion of epistemology).
- While it is not possible to synthesize these theories in order to foreground all sets of structural–agentic processes, it is possible to move between the interpretations offered by different theories in order to compare the understandings of teaching–learning interactions that they make possible (from the discussion of epistemology).
- Structural descriptions of teaching–learning interactions involve conceiving how they are shaped by structural–agentic processes as well as how such sets of processes are transformed by the particularities of teaching–learning interactions (from the discussion of relations between structural–agentic processes and teaching–learning interactions).
- Agentic descriptions of teaching–learning interactions are focused on conceiving the relations between the projects of those involved in terms of different sets of structural–agentic processes (from discussion of relations between structural–agentic processes and teaching–learning interactions).
- This means that the relations between particular sets of structural–agentic processes and teaching–learning interactions need to be conceived in two ways:
    - In structural terms, focusing on how particular sets of structural–agentic processes become situated in and shape teaching–learning interactions.
    - In agentic terms, focusing on how the dynamic relations between the projects of those involved in the teaching–learning interaction can be characterized in terms of the particular set of structural–agentic processes.

- As the ways of conceiving these relations are simplifications of complex social processes, they need to be interrogated and developed by being examined in relation to empirical data on teaching–learning interactions in higher education.

Conclusion

In this chapter I have set out a way of the accounting for structure and agency in teaching–learning interactions in higher education. This approach involves a focus on the relations between conceptualizations of particular sets of structural–agentic processes and teaching–learning interactions. The next stage in my argument is to consider ways of conceiving particular sets of structural–agentic processes that are significant in relation to teaching–learning interactions in higher education. It is to this task that I turn in the next chapter by examining the literature on teaching–learning processes in higher education. In doing so, I also examine the problems of drawing on this literature to analyse the relations between sets of structural–agentic processes and teaching–learning interactions in higher education.

Chapter 3

Current ways of analysing the relations between structural–agentic processes and teaching–learning interactions

In Chapter 2, I argued that accounting for structure and agency in teaching–learning interactions in higher education involves analysing the relations between such interactions and sets of structural–agentic processes. In this chapter, I first examine the ways of describing sets of structural–agentic processes that the existing literature on teaching–learning processes in higher education suggests are significant. I then examine how these different sets of structural–agentic processes are conceptualized in research into teaching–learning processes in higher education. I argue that the current mainstream approaches to research in this area do not meet the particular challenges of analysing the relations between these sets of structural–agentic processes and teaching–learning interactions. In particular, I argue that the tendency in research in this area to separate the perceptions and practices of students from the perceptions and practices of academics seriously hinders its capacity to account for these relations. For this reason, I argue that there is a need to examine alternative approaches to analysing the relations between sets of structural–agentic processes and teaching–learning interactions in higher education.

In making this argument it is important to be clear that my criticisms of the research I examine are criticisms of its capacity to examine the relations between sets of structural–agentic processes and teaching–learning interactions in higher education. It is important to recognize that this research has not been developed with the intention of dealing with this question. Therefore, it is not surprising that this research does not deal with the issue well and is not a criticism of this research *in its own terms*. My position is that the research I review in this chapter has added a great deal to the understanding of teaching–learning processes in higher education but that it is of more limited value when examining the relations between sets of structural–agentic processes and teaching–learning interactions.

Which characterizations of structural–agentic processes appear to be significant in relation to teaching–learning processes in higher education?

In Chapter 1, I outlined two dominant perspectives on researching teaching–learning processes in higher education: the Approaches to Learning and Teaching perspective and Social Practice perspectives. Despite differences in the ways in which teaching–learning processes are conceived in this research, there is remarkable consistency about the sets of structural–agentic processes that are argued to be significant. Papers that summarize such factors from both of these perspectives identify broadly the same sets of processes: the teaching–learning environment, the identities of academics and students, the disciplinary knowledge practices that are the focus of the interaction, and the cultures of the higher education institutions in which the interactions take place (for example, from the Approaches to Learning and Teaching perspective see Biggs 1993; Entwistle 2007; Ashwin and McLean 2005; from the social practices perspectives see Trowler 1998; 2008; Lea and Street 1998; and Fanghanel 2006). It is important to be clear that an implication of the argument that I have developed in Chapter 2 is that these are particular ways of characterizing sets of structural–agentic processes rather than teaching–learning environments, identities, disciplinary knowledge practices and institutional cultures being seen as existing in the social world and awaiting discovery by perceptive researchers.

While the exact makeup of the sets of agentic–structural processes are not always the same, the types of processes listed above tend to feature in some form. As this book marks an initial attempt to engage with the relations between sets of structural–agentic processes and teaching–learning interactions in higher education, it is these characterizations of sets of structural–agentic processes that I examine in the rest of this book. This is not to suggest that there are not other ways of characterizing sets of structural–agentic processes that might be important in teaching–learning processes. For example, Knight and Trowler (2000) argue strongly the departmental setting, as distinct from institutional or disciplinary settings, is crucial in shaping teaching–learning processes. Rather, in examining the relations between sets of structural–agentic processes and teaching–learning interactions, I will use these four sets of processes as exemplars. These sets of processes will be used as exemplars of the limitations of existing research into teaching–learning processes for analysing the relations between such processes and teaching–learning interactions. They will also be used to examine what other perspectives mght be helpful to analyse such relations.

In Chapter 2, I argued that there are two aspects of examining the relations between sets of structural–agentic processes and teaching–learning interactions. These are examining both how particular sets of structural–agentic processes become situated in the teaching–learning interaction, and how the teaching–learning interaction can be characterized in terms of the particular set of structural–agentic processes. For each set of structural–agentic processes, I first introduce a particular research perspective that has focused on characterizing that set of processes before examining its particular characterization. I then examine how that characterization deals with both the issue of how the set of structural–agentic processes is situated in the teaching–learning interaction and how the teaching–learning interaction is characterized in terms of the particular set of structural–agentic processes.

In doing so, my aim is not to offer a comprehensive review of all the literature relating to each set of processes; rather, I want to highlight the key issues in accounting for the relations between each set of structural–agentic processes and teaching–learning interactions. This approach has two implications. First, it means that I examine particular approaches to examining each set of structural–agentic processes as exemplars of what I argue are wider issues with the literature. Second, in doing so I am only focused on how each of these sets of structural–agentic processes relates to teaching–learning interactions in higher education. They clearly impact on other aspects of higher education, such as research and management, but my focus is limited to understanding their relations to teaching–learning interactions.

The teaching–learning environment in higher education

The teaching–learning environment in higher education has been most exhaustively researched from the Approaches to Learning and Teaching perspective; indeed, the dominance of this perspective has been criticized (Webb 1997; Malcolm and Zukas 2001; Haggis 2003). Given the dominance of this perspective, I focus on how it has characterized the teaching–learning environment in higher education.

The Approaches to Learning and Teaching perspective

The Approaches to Learning and Teaching perspective is made up of research from a phenomenographic and a cognitivist perspective (see Trigwell 2006; Åkerlind 2007; Greasley and Ashworth 2007 for discussions of the differences between these perspectives).

'Phenomenography' (see Marton and Booth 1997 for an introduction and history) was initially developed in Sweden in the 1970s. This has focused on examining the qualitative variation in the way in which groups of students or academics have experienced particular phenomena in higher education including 'learning' (see Marton and Säljö 1997), 'teaching' (see Prosser and Trigwell 1999), 'creativity in teaching and learning' (Kleiman 2007), and particular academic tasks (for example, see Hodgson 1997 on lectures; Laurillard 1997 on problem solving; Ashwin 2005, 2006b on tutorials). This research focuses on examining the qualitative different ways of experiencing these phenomena within a group. Thus it does not examine individuals' conceptions of these phenomena but rather examines the number of qualitatively different ways in which a particular phenomenon is experienced within a group. Phenomenographic data are usually generated using qualitative interviews (see Åkerlind 2005 for a discussion of phenomenographic methods), although it has been used to examine open-ended responses to questionnaire items (for example, see Åkerlind and Kayrooz 2003)

Approaches to Learning and Teaching research from a cognitive perspective was developed in the UK by the work of Entwistle and Ramsden in the late 1960s to the 1980s (see Entwistle and Ramsden 1983 as well as Entwistle 1987 and Entwistle 1988 for a history of this research) and by John Biggs in Australia (see Biggs 1979). This research was largely based on the development of inventory scales which examined students' approaches to learning. This research has also developed in mainland Europe (for example see Vermunt 2007) with crossovers with research into self-regulated learning in the US (for example, see Pintrich 2004) (see Richardson 2000 for a discussion of different types of inventories; and Entwistle and McCune 2004 for an examination of the conceptual basis of these inventories).

Rather than being separate, these two strands of the Approaches to Learning and Teaching perspective have developed in dialogue together. For example, work on academics' approaches to teaching has developed from both of these strands (for example, Martin and Balla 1991; Samuelowicz and Bain 1992; Gow and Kember 1993; Trigwell and Prosser 1996; Prosser and Trigwell 1999; Åkerlind 2003). What both of these strands have in common is that they are focused on how students' and academics' perceptions of the teaching–learning environment relate to the ways in which they approach teaching–learning processes in that environment and how these approaches relate to the outcomes of these processes.

The teaching–learning environment from the Approaches to Learning and Teaching perspective

The Approaches to Learning and Teaching perspective focuses on how students' and academics' perceptions of the teaching–learning environment structure their engagement in teaching–learning processes in higher education. In different studies in the Approaches to Learning and Teaching perspective the 'teaching–learning environment' varies in scope from a particular task (for example, see Laurillard 1997) to an entire programme (for example, see McCune and Hounsell 2005). However, whatever level is selected, the results tend to be similar. Research from this perspective suggests that where students perceive that their teaching is good, their workload is appropriate, the assessment is focused on assessing their understanding, and that the aims of their programmes are clear, then they are more likely to attempt to develop an understanding of what they are learning (a deep approach to learning) rather than simply reproduce knowledge for the sake of assessment (a surface approach to learning). Deep and surface approaches to learning have been argued to be consistently related to the quality of students' learning outcomes, with students who adopt a deep approach to learning more likely to achieve higher learning outcomes (for summaries, see Prosser and Trigwell 1999; Richardson 2005; Entwistle 2007; Vermunt 2007).

Similarly, where academics perceive that their class sizes are not too large, that they have control over their teaching, and that their teaching is valued by the institution, they are more likely to adopt an approach to teaching that is focused on changing students' conceptions of the material they are learning (a conceptual change/student-focused approach to teaching) rather than adopting an approach to teaching that is focused on the transmission (an information transfer/teacher-focused approach to teaching) (for summaries see Prosser and Trigwell 1999; Åkerlind 2003; Richardson 2005; Entwistle 2007).

Academics' approaches to teaching have also been argued to relate to students' approaches to learning. The students of academics who report adopting an information transfer/teacher-focused approach to teaching are more likely to adopt a surface approach to learning, whereas the students of academics who report adopting a conceptual change/student-focused approach to teaching are more likely to adopt a deep approach to learning (Trigwell *et al.* 1999).

Thus research from the Approaches to Learning and Teaching perspective has suggested that there are consistent relations between students' and academics' perceptions of the teaching–learning environment, and the quality and outcomes of teaching–learning processes. It is also argued that where students do not have any clear perception of their teaching–learning environment (a disintegrated or dissonant approach to learning), then they tend to perform more poorly than students who adopt a surface approach (see for example, Meyer and Vermunt 2000). The same has been argued in relation to academics' perceptions of the teaching–learning environment (see for example, Prosser *et al.* 2003).

This research has increasingly moved from a focus on students' and academics' general approaches to learning–teaching processes in higher education, to focus on how teaching–learning processes are approached in particular kinds of environments. This has included a focus on how teaching–learning environments are structured in particular disciplines, for example in the recent work on 'ways of thinking and practising in the disciplines' (Anderson and Day 2005; Entwistle 2005; McCune and Hounsell 2005; Anderson and Hounsell 2007; Hounsell and Hounsell 2007), work on how the structure of disciplinary knowledge impacts on students' learning through research into threshold concepts (Meyer and Land 2005; Davies and Mangan 2007;

Lucas and Mladenovic 2007; Perkins 2007) and the 'new' phenomenography (Marton 2007), research into disciplinary differences in approaches to teaching (Lindblom-Ylänne *et al.* 2006) and how academics' understanding of their disciplines impacts on their teaching (Martin *et al.* 2002; Prosser *et al.* 2007). There has also been work on how institutional contexts impact on students' learning through the Social Organisation and Mediation of University Learning (SOMUL) project (Brennan and Jary 2005; Brennan and Osborne 2005a,b, 2008; Houston and Lebeau 2006; Richardson and Edmunds 2007), the National Student Survey (Richardson *et al.* 2007) and the use of the Course Experience Questionnaire (CEQ) in Australia (Ramsden 1991; McInnis *et al.* 2001).

This focus on particular teaching–learning environments has led to the use of other theoretical tools to supplement the work of the Approaches to Learning and Teaching perspective. For example, the SOMUL project has drawn on Bernstein (see Brennan and Osborne 2005a,b), while some of the literature on 'ways of thinking and practising in the disciplines' situates itself in a socio-cultural perspective (for example see Anderson and Day 2005). However, the focus is still very much on students' and academics' experiences of the teaching–learning environment and, as is the case with the two examples given, the research still tends to draw upon inventories developed from the Approaches to Learning and Teaching perspective.

The possibilities and tensions of an Approaches to Learning and Teaching analysis of the relations between teaching–learning environments and teaching–learning interactions

How does the Approaches to Learning and Teaching perspective deal with the two aspects of analysing the relations between structural–agentic processes and teaching–learning interactions that I outlined earlier? In relation to how the teaching–learning environment is conceived as becoming situated in the teaching–learning interaction, it does not appear to focus on how the teaching–learning environment is produced in particular teaching–learning interactions. Instead, it focuses on students' and academics' perceptions of an already existing teaching–learning environment, so there is no focus on the processes that led to the production of that environment. Thus, in focusing on students' and academics' perceptions of the teaching–learning environment, there is little sense given of how that environment itself is situated within the teaching–learning interaction.

In relation to the second set of questions about how the teaching–learning interaction is characterized in terms of the teaching–learning environment, it does not provide a sense of the dynamic and interactive aspects of teaching–learning processes. Rather, as I have outlined in Chapter 1, it tends to either focus on academics' perceptions of teaching or students' perceptions of learning. This gives little sense of the way in which academics and students continually impact on each other in particular interactions. As a result, when the relations between academics' approaches to teaching and students' approaches to learning are examined, they are linked in a fairly distant manner, largely through the examination of the relation between students' and academics' scores on questionnaire inventories (for example, see Trigwell *et al.* 1999; Vermunt and Verloop 1999) (see Ashwin 2008 for a development of this argument).

In summary, although the Approaches to Learning and Teaching perspective contributes to an understanding of the relations between academics' and students' perceptions of the teaching–learning environment and their approaches to, and outcomes from, learning and teaching, it does not really help in an analysis of the ways in which the teaching–learning environment is produced within particular teaching–learning interactions, or how teaching–learning interactions can be characterized in terms of the teaching–learning environment. In Chapter 4, I examine whether Engeström's (2001) version of Activity Theory offers a more helpful way of analysing these relations.

The identities of academics and students

The second characterization of a set of structural–agentic processes that I examine is the identities of academics and students. Issues of identity in relation to teaching–learning processes in higher education have largely been examined from within a range of Social Practice perspectives. Identities are seen as central to discussions of Communities of Practice (for example, Wenger 1998 argues that practice entails negotiated ways of being a person); research examining alienation and engagement in higher education (Mann 2001, 2005; Case 2008);

research examining student identities as complex systems (Haggis 2006) and also from an Academic Literacies perspective. In discussing research foregrounding the identities of academics and students, I will focus on research from an Academic Literacies perspective for two reasons. First, because of its focus on how identities are developed through literacy practices, it tends to focus specifically on how identities are constructed in relation to teaching–learning processes in higher education. Second, because it is often posited as the strongest alternative to the Approaches to Teaching and Learning perspective (for example, see Haggis 2003, 2004).

The Academic Literacies perspective

Work on Academic Literacies in higher education (Lea and Street 1998) can be seen to have developed from New Literacy Studies (for example, see Street 1984; Baynham 1995; Barton and Hamilton 1998; as well as Barton 2007 for a brief history).

As its name suggests, an Academic Literacies perspective is primarily focused on how identities are developed through reading and writing practices. In this way literacy is seen primarily as something people do rather than something that is located in people's heads (Barton and Hamilton 1998). Within research from an Academic Literacies perspective, people are seen as engaging in distinct discourse communities in different domains of their lives, where domains are seen as structured, patterned contexts that involve fairly regular sets of literacy practices. These practices are structured and sustained by particular institutions (Barton and Hamilton 1998). This means that literacy practices in higher education are seen as a particular kind of literacy practice bound up with the workings of a social institution (Lillis 2001). Further, as Lea and Street (1998, 2006) argue, different academic settings in higher education draw on different literacy practices. Thus rather than higher education being relatively homogenous, it is characterized by different epistemologies that require students to develop different kinds of identities. These identities are different both in terms of the identities that students develop in relation to literacy practices outside of higher education (for example, see Mann 2000 on the students' experiences of the differences between reading for pleasure and reading for their higher education programmes) and in terms of the identities developed in different disciplinary and institutional contexts (Lea and Street 1998, 2006; Hermerschmidt 1999)

So in contrast to the Approaches to Learning and Teaching, an Academic Literacies perspective foregrounds the ways in which students and academics develop identities and practices in relation to particular institutional and disciplinary settings rather than foregrounding how they perceive the teaching–learning environment.

The identities of academics and students from an Academic Literacies perspective

As I argued in the introduction to this section, Academic Literacies research examines how identities are developed through literacy practices in higher education. In this way, it can be seen to focus on how identities are constructed in relation to teaching–learning processes in higher education. For example, Ivanič (1998) examines the experience of eight mature students as they construct identities through writing processes and the options that appeared to be available for selfhood in the academic community. Similarly, Lillis (1999, 2001) examines the sorts of identities that non-traditional students are able to develop in their writing in relation to particular institutional and disciplinary forms of higher education.

Thus an Academic Literacies view of identity focuses on how identity is performed through particular practices and how factors such as students' class, race and gender lead them to be positioned in particular ways in relation to the teaching–learning environment, particular disciplines and institutional processes. As Hamilton (2001) argues, an Academic Literacies perspective highlights the need to understand how institutions produce and privilege certain kinds of knowing.

Although work from an Academic Literacies perspective has generally focused on *students'* literacy practices, this view of identity is also consistent with work that has examined academics' identities in relation to teaching–learning processes. For example, Henkel's (2000) research on academic identities, which includes a consideration of teaching identities, is based on a view of identities as changeable but limited by the institutions and communities of which academics are members. While Sikes (2006) questions the emphasis that Henkel places on disciplines in shaping academic identities, her view of the process by which identities were constructed is broadly similar. Similarly, Jawitz (2007) argues that the identity trajectories of academic staff are shaped by their individual histories and experiences as well as their institutional context, while others focus on how gender, class and race impact on the construction and experience of academic identities (for example, see Reay 2000, 2004; Anderson and Williams 2001; Bhopal 2002; Mackie 2006; Clegg 2008b).

The possibilities and tensions of an Academic Literacies analysis of the relations between students' and academics' identities and teaching–learning interactions

An Academic Literacies analysis of the relations between students' and academics' identities and teaching–learning interactions provides a sense of how such identities become situated in teaching–learning interactions. It provides both a sense of the origins of these identities as well as how these identities are reshaped as they are situated in particular teaching–learning interactions (for example, see Ivanič 1998; Lillis 1999, 2001).

However, in relation to how it offers a way of characterizing the dynamic and shifting aspects of teaching–learning interactions in terms of the identities of students and academics, it again proves problematic. This is because it is clear that the literacy practices of an academic teaching are different from the literacy practices of students engaged in learning tasks. This can make it difficult to gain a sense of how the identities of academics and students continually impact on each other within teaching–learning interactions. Rather, the focus tends to be on the overall relations between the different world-views of the student and academics without a sense of how these come together to create particular identities in particular interactions.

In summary, while the Academic Literacies perspective foregrounds how students' and academics' identities in teaching–learning interactions relate to their other identities, it again does not foreground the ways in which the dynamic aspects of teaching–learning interactions can be characterized in terms of academics' and students' identities. In Chapter 5, I examine Symbolic Interactionism as a way of analysing the relations between student and academic identities and teaching–learning interactions.

Disciplinary knowledge practices

There has been extensive work on the impact of the disciplines on teaching–learning processes in higher education. When referring to disciplines as a set of structural–agentic processes, I use the term 'disciplinary knowledge practices' to emphasize them as dynamic processes rather than static things (see Anderson and Hounsell 2007 for a similar use of terminology)

Trowler (2008b) argues that much of the work on the disciplinary knowledge practices has been informed by 'epistemological essentialism', the notion that disciplinary knowledge practices *determine* teaching–learning processes (see Trowler and Wareham 2007 for a review of the different positions developed in relation to the impact of disciplinary knowledge practices on teaching–learning processes). In what Trowler (in press) cites as the most widely known example of 'epistemological essentialism', Becher (1989) argues that this is both related to the structures of knowledge and the social structures within disciplines. This work has been further developed in relation to teaching–learning processes in higher education by Neumann (Neumann 2001; Neumann *et al.* 2002) and also within more quantitative work, particularly in the US, examining disciplinary differences in teaching–learning processes (see for example, Brint *et al.* 2008; Nelson Laird *et al.* 2008).

Trowler (in press) and Becher and Trowler (2001) argue that this approach overstates the power of disciplinary knowledge practices to shape teaching–learning processes. This is partly because of the impact of other factors such as the identities of academics and the institutional cultures in which these processes are situated, but also because, in the words of Becher and Trowler (2001, pp. 29–30), rather than 'a seamless cloak':

> knowledge would appear more closely comparable with a badly made patchwork quilt, some of whose constituents are only loosely tacked together, while others untidily overlap, and yet others seem inadvertently to have been omitted, leaving large and shapeless gaps in the fabric of the whole.

This view of disciplinary knowledge practices is supported by research examining the experiences of research and teaching–learning processes in particular disciplines. For example, Evans (1993) argues that as a discipline English is more of an archipelago than a landmass and suggests that it is only when different disciplines are compared that they take on the appearance of homogeneity.

In examining how the relations between disciplinary knowledge practices and teaching–learning interactions have been analysed in higher education research, I focus on work from a Communities of Practice perspective. Tight (2008) discusses the relative strengths of conceiving of disciplinary knowledge practices as 'Tribes and Territories' or in terms of 'Communities of Practice', while Becher and Parry (2005) argue that focusing on academic Communities of Practice moves away from focusing on the cognitive structure of pure disciplines to the social organization of more interdisciplinary subjects. My reason for drawing on the notion of Communities of Practice rather than 'Tribes and Territories' is that I am examining these disciplinary knowledge practices in relation to teaching–learning interactions, and a Communities of Practice perspective seems more suitable for this purpose because it is explicitly based on a theory of learning.

The Communities of Practice perspective

Communities of Practice research shares many of the same initial reference points as Academic Literacies. Barton and Hamilton (2005, p. 14) argue that 'The two approaches have common roots in the work of Scribner and Cole (1981), but then the fields of situated learning and situated literacies largely developed separately.' Recently there have been a number of attempts to bring the two together (for example, Barton and Tursting 2005 and in relation to higher education specifically Lea 2005 and Tummons 2008).

Given these common roots, it is not surprising that the two perspectives have a good deal in common. Both focus on the relation between practices and identity within particular communities. For example, Wenger (2000) argues that Communities of Practice consist of a domain, a set of shared practices and a community. The similarity to Barton and Hamilton's (1998) approach to discourse communities, which I outlined earlier, is striking. As the above quote from Barton and Hamilton (2005) suggests, the difference lies in the focus on how learning, rather than literacy, is situated within particular domains in the Communities of Practice literature.

Within the view of learning in Communities of Practice research, the focus is on everyday interactions, which means that there is no separation of learning from other activities (Lave 1993) and learning is seen as a way of being in the social world (Gherardi *et al.* 1998). This means that learning is seen as an embodied, rather than simply a cognitive, activity (Hammersley 2005). People develop meanings within these interactions, which means understandings emerge in the processes of practice (Lave 1993) and, to some extent, they have a 'local' meaning (Brown and Duguid 1991). These understandings are collective and a product of the community rather than individuals (Brown and Duguid 1991; Lave 1993; Gherardi *et al.* 1998) and people are seen to learn by access to and membership of these Communities of Practice (Lave and Wenger 1991).

In this way Wenger (1998, p. 45, emphasis in the original) argues that:

> Over time . . . collective learning results in practices that reflect both the pursuit of our enterprises and the attendant social relations. These practices are thus the property of a community created over time by the sustained pursuit of a shared enterprise. It makes sense, therefore, to call these kinds of communities *communities of practice.*

Disciplinary knowledge practices from a Communities of Practice perspective

A number of studies of teaching–learning processes in higher education argue that the disciplinary knowledge practices can be conceptualized from a Communities of Practice perspective. In relation to teaching, Healey (2005) and Lucas (2007) have used the notion to examine the relations between research and teaching in particular disciplines. In relation to learning, Shreeve (2007) has examined learning processes in Art and Design using the idea of Communities of Practice, Dahlgren *et al.* (2006) have used it to examine the transition between higher education and work in different disciplines, and Solomon (2007) uses the idea to examine students' identity formation in Math-

ematics. In relation to assessment, the idea of disciplinary Communities of Practice has been used in a series of studies by Price, O'Donovan and Rust (Price 2005; O'Donovan *et al.* 2004; Price *et al.* 2007) to
examine how academics and students come to understand assessment
criteria, while Shay (2004) and Jawitz (2007) uses it to investigate how
academics approach the assessment of complex tasks.

In analysing disciplinary knowledge practices in this way, it is clear
that a disciplinary community of practice is just one of a number of
communities of practice that students and academics might belong to.
Solomon (2007) argues that Mathematics students as well as being part
of the community of their discipline are, among others, also members
of the general undergraduate community, and that there were conflicts between the values of the different communities of practice of
which they were members. James (2007) argues that academics are
members of multiple communities of practice that again are potentially conflicting, while Price (2005) argues that academic staff will
draw on departmental, as well as their disciplinary communities, when
assessing students' work.

One of the attractions of thinking about the disciplinary knowledge
practices in terms of Communities of Practice is that it offers a way of
conceptualizing students and academics as members of the *same* community. The academic can be seen as offering students, as peripheral
but legitimate members of the community, a way of increasingly
moving towards the centre of the disciplinary community. For this
reason, Parker (2002) and Brew (2006) draw on the idea of Communities of Practice in arguing for the development of knowledge-
building communities in higher education that include both students
and academics.

The possibilities and tensions of a Communities of Practice analysis of the relations between disciplinary knowledge practices and teaching–learning interactions

How does a Communities of Practice perspective deal with the two
aspects of analysing the relations between structural–agentic processes
and teaching–learning interactions? In relation to how disciplinary
knowledge practices become situated in teaching–learning interactions, it appears to assume that they enter into the teaching–learning

interaction in an unmediated way. Thus it appears to assume that the discipline-as-research is the same as the discipline-as-curriculum, in that the knowledge practices of research activities in a particular discipline are assumed to be the same as the knowledge practices involved in the higher education curricula related to that discipline. In this way, it tends to obscure the processes by which disciplinary knowledge practices become situated in teaching–learning interactions in higher education.

In relation to how the dynamic and shifting aspects of teaching–learning interactions can be characterized in terms of disciplinary knowledge practices, it again seems to offer little assistance. This is because it either will assume that students and academics are part of the same or different Communities of Practices. If it assumes they are part of different Communities of Practice, then it suffers from the same problem that I identified in relation to an Academic Literacies. This is that if students and academics are engaged in different practices as part of different communities, then it is difficult to get a sense of how they interact. This can be gained by seeing students and academics as part of the same community. However, this raises the question of what are the practices that students and academics share? As I indicated earlier, this is sometimes characterized in terms of academics supporting students to become members of their disciplinary Communities of Practice. The problem is that not only does this again assume that the practices of the discipline-as-research are the same as the practices of the discipline-as-curriculum, it also involves the assumption that programmes of study in higher education are focused on preparing the next generation of researchers, academics or professionals in relation to particular disciplinary knowledge practices. This seems an inappropriate assumption in a mass system of higher education, where students' career choices often bear no direct relation to the disciplines they study and given the evidence that students do not feel part of the disciplinary knowledge practice communities related to their programmes of study (Solomon 2007; Brennan and Osborne 2008). Thus the two possible ways of characterizing teaching–learning interactions from the perspective of disciplinary knowledge practices offered by a Communities of Practices do not appear to be helpful.

In summary, the Communities of Practice perspective does not really help in trying to understand the processes through which disciplinary knowledge practices become situated in teaching–learning interactions, the processes through which disciplines-as-research are transformed into disciplines-as-curriculum. It also does not provide a helpful way of characterizing teaching–learning interactions in terms of disciplinary knowledge practices. In Chapter 6, I examine how Bernstein's (1990, 2000) conception of the pedagogic device might provide an alternative way of conceiving of the relations between disciplinary knowledge practices and teaching–learning interactions.

Institutional cultures

As Jenkins (2004) notes in relation to research-teaching relations, there has been far less research into the impact of institutional cultures on teaching–learning processes in higher education than there has been on the impact of disciplinary knowledge practices. As was noted earlier, there have been comparisons of how different institutions perform on the Course Experience Questionnaire and on other measures of academic quality (for example, see Ramsden 1991; McInnis *et al.* 2001) but this has examined differences in the way in which students' perceive the teaching–learning environment in different institutions rather than exploring the way in which institutional cultures relate to teaching–learning processes. Equally, many studies have examined the differences between the organizational cultures in different universities (for example, de Zilwa 2007). As Välimaa (1998) and Yorke (2004) note, such research is more common in the US than in the UK and Europe, a difference that Yorke (2004) puts down to greater competition between institutions in the US. This research tends to focus on institutional cultures generally (for example, see Tierney 1988 for a classic framework of organizational cultures and Trowler 2008a for a review of different approaches) rather than how these cultures impact on teaching–learning processes, even if some research has considered how such cultures impact on the introduction of learning initiatives (see Kezar *et al.* 2008 for a summary).

There are a number of studies that suggest that institutional cultures are important in teaching–learning processes. In relation to student experiences, Yorke and Longden (2007) argued that there were little differences in first-year experiences between pre- and post-1992 institutions as types but that there were clear differences between different institutions. In the US, Kezar (2006) argued that size of institution had an impact on the ways in which students engaged in teaching–learning processes. In relation to assessment, Gibbs and Dunbar-Goddett (2007) argued that differences in approaches to assessment on different programmes were more related to institutional differences than disciplinary differences.

Studies of teaching–learning processes in relation to particular disciplinary knowledge practices tend also to be sensitive to differences in institutional cultures. While Jones *et al.* (2005) argued that there were little differences in the English that was produced in two different institutional cultures, the ways in which it was produced did differ. As I argued in Chapter 1, for a variety of reasons students from different social classes tend to attend different types of higher education institutions (Ashworth 2004; Brennan and Osborne 2008; Crozier *et al.* 2008), which may also have an impact on institutional cultures. Henkel (2000) argued that there were similar differences in her examination of academic identities in different universities.

This suggests a picture of institutions of different sizes, with different intakes of students in terms of prior academic achievement and social class and race, studying different curricula and being assessed in different ways. However, Trowler and Knight (1999) argue that it is too simplistic to see such differences simply in terms of differences in top-down institutional cultures. They use the notion of multiple cultural configurations (for example, see Alvesson 2002) to argue that there are sets of cultures that at the level of the teaching–learning processes take on particular kinds of meanings. Such cultures are local versions of wider societal cultures, institutional and departmental cultures, which can be seen to contradict and to be in conflict with each other. For example, Trowler (1998) argues that institutional factors play out differently in different departmental settings in the introduction of a new credit framework. Given that my focus is on the relations between institutional cultures and teaching–learning interactions, I use the later development of these ideas into the notion of 'Teaching and Learning Regimes' by Paul Trowler and his colleagues as a way of analysing these relations.

The Teaching and Learning Regimes (TLRs) perspective

The notion of 'Teaching and Learning Regimes' (TLRs) is focused at
the level of individual departments or workgroups within universities
(Trowler and Cooper 2002; Trowler 2005; Trowler *et al.* 2005; Trowler
2008a). A TLR is a:

> constellation of rules, assumptions, practices and relationships
> related to teaching and learning issues in higher education . . . In
> deploying the term 'regime' we draw attention to social relationships
> and recurrent practices, the technologies that instantiate them (room
> layouts and pedagogic techniques) and the ideologies, values, and
> attitudes that underpin them. (Trowler and Cooper 2002, p. 224)

Institutional cultures from a Teaching and Learning Regimes perspective

The concept of Teaching and Learning Regimes is an attempt to
analyse the ways in which institutional cultures impact on attempts to
improve teaching–learning processes in higher education. Initiatives
are seen to play out differently because they are filtered through different cultural components, or, as Trowler (2005, 2008a) calls them,
'moments'. These moments include the 'tacit assumptions'; 'implicit
theories of teaching and learning'; 'recurrent practices'; 'conventions
of appropriateness'; 'discursive repertoires'; 'power relations'; 'subjec-
tivities in interaction'; and 'codes of signification' of particular departments or workgroups (see Trowler and Cooper 2002; Trowler 2005;
Trowler *et al.* 2005; Trowler 2008a). Trowler (2005, 2008a) is clear that
these moments need to be seen holistically and that they can be only
separated analytically.

It is through these moments that Trowler (2005, 2008a) attempts to
address the lack of focus on power within a Communities of Practice
perspective and the related tendency to imply that workgroups operate
in a consensual manner. Trowler and Cooper (2002) use these ideas
to examine differences between the TLRs of academic development
programmes and the TLRs of participants' departments. They argue
that incompatibilities in these TLRs prevent such development programmes leading to changes in teaching–learning practices within the

participants' departments. Trowler *et al.* (2005) examine how national and institutional policies are filtered through different TLRs. Fanghanel (2004, 2006, 2007) has made similar arguments from a related standpoint. My suggestion is that a TLR can also be used to consider how particular institutional cultures are filtered through the 'regimes' related to particular teaching–learning interactions.

The possibilities and tensions of a Teaching Learning Regimes analysis of the relations between institutional cultures and teaching–learning interactions

In relation to the first aspect of relating structural–agentic processes and teaching–learning interactions, the TLR perspective gives a clear sense of how institutional cultures become situated in particular teaching–learning interactions. It provides a focus on how institutional cultures are filtered through the cultural moments in which the particular interaction is situated and gives a sense of how the meaning of the many facets of institutional cultures discussed above (the nature and size of the student body, the physical environment, institutional policies etc.) is partially shaped by the TLRs in which it operates. Thus it gives an excellent sense of how similar institutional cultures can take on completely different meanings and have different effects depending on the TLRs into which it is introduced. However, while it gives a sense of how institutional structural–agentic processes are shaped by the particular locale and how they are refracted through the filters of a particular situation, it does not give an initial sense of what these institutional cultures might be. This means that it does not provide a sense of where institutional cultures, or differences in institutional cultures, originate from.

In relation to how teaching–learning interactions can be characterized from the perspective of institutional cultures, it focuses on the impact of refracted institutional cultures on the practices of academics. In drawing on the idea of the practices of academics and students, it again separates students and academics because of the clear differences of their practices within teaching–learning processes. Thus it does not provide a sense of how the dynamic and shifting aspects of teaching–learning interactions can be characterized in terms of institutional cultures.

In summary, although the TLR gives a good sense of the processes that situate institutional cultures in relation to particular teaching–learning interactions, it does not help to conceptualize what those institutional processes might be or how teaching–learning interactions might be characterized in terms of institutional cultures. In Chapter 7, I examine how Bourdieu's notions of 'field', 'capital' and '*habitus*' might provide an alternative way of analysing the relations between institutional cultures and teaching–learning interactions in higher education.

Conclusion

In this chapter I have examined a number of ways of analysing teaching–learning processes in higher education. In each case, while each of the perspectives has much to offer, they have particular short-comings when focusing on the relations between particular character-izations of sets of structural–agentic processes and teaching–learning interactions. While some of the perspectives give a sense of how sets of structural–agentic processes are situated in teaching–learning interac-tions in higher education, none offered a way of conceptualizing the dynamic and shifting aspects of teaching–learning interactions. This, I argued, was because of the way in which they draw on the notions of students' and academics' perceptions or practices to inform their analyses. In different ways, both of these notions encourage a separa-tion of the activities of students and academics within teaching–learning interactions, a separation which obscures the dynamic and shifting aspects of such interactions.

In Chapters 4 to 7 of this book, I examine alternative ways of analysing these relationships, which although common in research relating to teaching–learning processes outside of universities, are less commonly used in examining teaching–learning processes in higher education.

Chapter 4

Analysing the relations between teaching–learning environments and teaching–learning interactions

Introduction

In this chapter I examine Engeström's (2001) version of Activity Theory as a way of analysing the relations between teaching–learning environments and teaching–learning interactions in higher education. I first outline my reasons for examining Activity Theory before introducing it more fully as a perspective. I then examine the different ways in which the teaching–learning environments can be conceptualized from the perspective of Activity Theory before examining how it supports an analysis of the relations between teaching–learning environments and teaching–learning interactions. This involves examining both how it gives a sense of the way in which teaching–learning environments become situated in teaching–learning interactions and how the teaching–learning interactions can be characterized in terms of teaching–learning environments. Finally, I explore the possibilities and tensions of adopting Engeström's version of Activity Theory as a way of analysing the relations between teaching–learning environments and teaching–learning interactions in higher education.

Why use Activity Theory to analyse the relations between teaching–learning environments and teaching–learning interactions in higher education?

In Chapter 3, I argued that teaching–learning environments in higher education have mainly been conceptualized through the Approaches to Learning and Teaching perspective. I argued that this perspective foregrounds the relations between students' and academics' perceptions of teaching–learning environments and their approaches to, and outcomes from, teaching–learning processes, rather than focusing on the relations between teaching–learning environments and teaching–

learning interactions. I argued that this focus means that the Approaches to Learning and Teaching perspective does not support an analysis of how teaching–learning environments are initially produced in teaching–learning interactions or the way in which teaching–learning interactions can be characterized in terms of teaching–learning environments.

The reason for examining an Activity Theory perspective is that it has an explicit focus on linking structural–agentic processes:

> The fundamental societal relations and contradictions of the given socio-economic formation – and thus potentials for qualitative change – are present in each and every local activity of that society. And vice versa, the mightiest, most impersonal societal structure can be seen as consisting of local activities carried out by concrete human beings with the help of mediating artefacts . . . In this sense it might be useful to try and look at the society more as a multi-layered network of interconnected activity systems and less as a pyramid of rigid structures dependent on a single center of power. (Engeström 1999b, pp. 8–9)

In this chapter I argue that this way of thinking about interacting activity systems provides a way of conceptualizing how teaching–learning environments are situated within teaching–learning interactions as well as how teaching–learning interactions can be characterized in terms of teaching–learning environments.

Engeström's Activity Theory

Engeström (2001) sees his work as part of the third generation of Activity Theory. The first generation, of which Vygotsky's (1978, 1986) work was the most significant, focused on the way in which tools or artefacts mediated the relation between subjects and objects; that is, the ways in which people use mediating artefacts to achieve their ends and the ways in which these artefacts impact on the consciousness of the people who use them. Thus language is an artefact that we can use to express ourselves, but it also shapes the terms in which we can talk and think. I will use the term 'mediating artefact' rather than 'tool' because, as Cole (1996) argues, the term 'mediating artefacts' is broader than that of tools because it can include people as well as concepts or material objects (see Leadbetter 2004 for an exploration of different types of mediating artefacts).

The second generation of Activity Theory, Engeström situates in the work of Leont'ev (1978). For Engeström, Leont'ev placed Vygotsky's ideas in a collective context by distinguishing between 'action' and 'activity'. Activity describes how people engage in collective tasks, with an intention that goes beyond the object of individual actions. The example that Leont'ev (1978) uses is of communal fishing where the overall objective of the collective activity is to get food, but the individual actions of, for example, repairing and preparing the nets in order to catch the fish are not directly related to getting food.

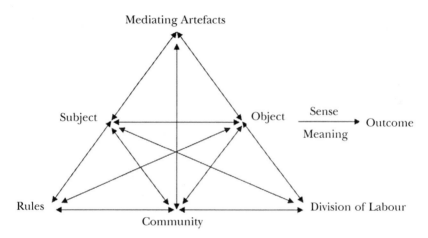

Figure 4.1: An activity system.
(Based on Engeström 2001, adapted and reprinted with the permission of the publisher: Taylor & Francis Ltd, www.tandf.co.uk/journals/titles/13639080.asp)

Figure 4.1 is Engeström's (2001) representation of Leont'ev's version of Activity Theory. Engeström (1996, p. 67) explains the diagram in the following way:

> . . . the *subject* refers to the individual or subgroup whose agency is chosen as the point of view in the analysis. The *object* refers to the 'raw material' or 'problem space' at which the activity is directed and which is molded or transformed into *outcomes* with the help of physical and symbolic, external or internal *tools* (mediating instruments and signs) [labelled 'mediating artefacts']. The *community*

comprises multiple individuals and/or subgroups who share the same general object. The *division of labor* refers to both the horizontal division of tasks between members of the community and to the vertical division of power and status. Finally, the *rules* refer to the explicit and implicit regulations, norms and conventions that constrain actions and interactions within the activity system. Between the components of an activity system, continuous construction is going on (e.g. agents modify tools, rules etc.).

The third generation of Activity Theory, where Engeström (2001) situates his work, focuses on a minimum of two interacting activity systems. This focus emphasizes the multi-voiced nature of activity. For example, Engeström (2001) reports on a project that was focused on getting greater understanding between the activity systems of hospital physicians, general practitioners and patients and their families in order to improve the system as a whole. In focusing on two or more activity systems interacting together, Engeström (2001) argues that the objects of the two activities system can change and lead to 'expansive learning'.

In summary, although, as in inevitable in developing a theory, Engeström's view of the crucial aspects of an activity system has changed (cf. Engeström 1987; 1996; 1999a,b; 2001), the key aspects of Engeström's view of Activity Theory can be summarized as:

1. The activity system as a whole should be taken as the unit of analysis. In doing so, there is a rejection of the separation of individual perception and situated action from the activity system as a whole.
2. Activity systems take shape and are formed over lengthy periods of time. Thus they have a history that shapes the way the activity is organized.
3. Because they are collective, activity systems are made up of a multitude of voices and perspectives that can be in conflict with each other.
4. Those involved in activity systems move from the internalization of the aspects of the activity system, which allows for the reproduction of culture, and externalization, in which they create new artefacts with the potential to lead to cultural change. As Engeström

(1999a) argues, those involved in an activity system shift from the internalization they need to become competent members of the activity to externalization through which individual innovations can change the activity system.

5. Activity systems develop and change through contradictions within a particular activity system and between activity systems.

6. These contradictions can be collectively harnessed by those within an activity system in order to generate expansive learning and this can be encouraged by a developmental research agenda. Thus for Engeström, following Marx, the point of coming to understand activity systems is in order to change them. This involves the researcher shifting from an objective view of the activity system to the view of the activity system of the actors involved, with the purpose of developing the activity system as a whole:

> Activity system as a unit of analysis calls for the complementarity of the system view and the subject's view. The analyst constructs the activity system as if looking at it from above. At the same time, the analyst must select a subject member (or better yet, multiple different members) of the local activity through whose eyes and interpretations the activity is constructed. The dialectic between the systematic and subjective-partisan views brings the researcher into a dialogical relationship with the local activity under investigation. (Engeström and Miettinen 1999, p. 10)

Conceptualizing teaching–learning environments from an Activity Theory perspective

Defining the teaching–learning environment

In examining how to conceptualize teaching–learning environments in terms of activity systems, it is important to be clear that within an activity system approach it is for the researcher to define what counts as the activity system, depending on the focus of their research (Russell 2002). In thinking about how Activity Theory can be drawn upon to analyse the relations between the structural–agentic processes of teaching–learning environments and teaching–learning interactions, there are two options.

First, one could define the teaching–learning environment itself as an activity system. This is the approach that is often taken in research in higher education as well as in other educational contexts, where programmes or modules are seen as the activity system (see for example, Knight *et al.* 2006; Barab *et al.* 2002; Russell 2002; Coupland and Crawford 2002; Berglund 2004; Havnes 2004; Mwenza and Engeström 2005). However, this option does not allow a focus on the ways in which students and academics interact within teaching–learning environments. This is because either the activity system would be examined from the perspective of the students or pupils (see for example, Engeström 1990; Berglund 2004; Havnes 2004; Scanlen and Issroff 2005), or from the perspective of the academics or teachers (see for example, Engeström 1994; Knight *et al.* 2006; Yamagata-Lynch 2003; Fanghanel 2004), or include both students and academics or pupils and teachers in the same activity system (see for example, Coupland and Crawford 2002; Mwenza and Engeström 2005). The first two clearly do not allow one to examine the way in which students and academics impact on each other in teaching–learning environments. The problem with the third approach is similar to the problem identified in relation to Communities of Practice in Chapter 3. This is that it does not seem intuitively correct that academics/teachers and students/pupils are engaged in the same activity system. Within higher education, it is not clear that students and academics have the same 'object' in teaching–learning interactions, that they are subject to the same 'rules' or that their activities are carried out in relation to the same 'community'. For example, academics' activity is likely to be situated in the community of the rest of their department or disciplinary group (for example, see Henkel 2000), while the relevant community for students might consist of other students (for example, see Solomon 2007). This point is supported by the differences in the activity systems generated from the perspective of students/pupils and those generated from the perspective of academics/teachers cited above.

Given this, and more in line with Engeström's (2001) focus on interacting activity systems, a second option would be to see student and academics as part of two different activity systems. Gutiérrez *et al.* (1999) argue that teaching–learning environments of classrooms are polycontextual in that they are made of multiple and connected activity systems. Based on this, they examine the multiple activity systems through which local and official knowledge discourses in schools can lead to expansive learning. Similarly Hakkarainen's (1999) analysis of the interacting activity systems of young children and day-care staff in a nursery suggests that conceptualizing teachers/academics and pupils/students as part of different activity systems allows an exploration of the different objects that they are focused upon in a single interaction. A focus on interacting activity systems has been adopted in research into higher education but more in terms of the different activity systems that academics (see Knight *et al.* 2006; Fanghanel 2004; Shreeve 2008) or students (see Russell and Yañez 2002) are involved in rather than the interactions between the activity systems of academics and students.

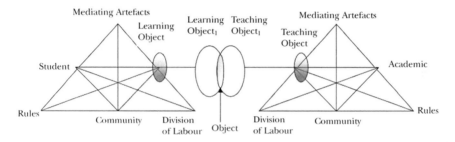

Figure 4.2: An initial sketch of teaching–learning environments as the interacting activity systems of students and academics.

(Based on Engeström 2001, adapted and reprinted with the permission of the publisher: Taylor & Francis Ltd, www.tandf.co.uk/journals/titles/13639080.asp)

Figure 4.2 is based on Engeström's (2001) illustration of what the two interacting systems might look like. It shows the activity systems of an academic and a student and shows how these systems might involve different mediating artefacts, draw up different rules, are situated with reference to different communities and involve a different division of labour. Crucially, it demonstrates that the object of the interaction may be different for the academic and for the student (the shaded ovals of 'Learning Object' and 'Teaching Object'). As the student and academic engage in the teaching–learning interactions, their view of what the object of their interaction is then changes (Learning Object 1 and Teaching Object 1). This *might* involve the development of a Shared Object (Object 3). However, it might not, and the student and the academic might not develop a shared object within the interaction, in which case the ovals would not overlap. This way of conceptualizing the teaching–learning environment gives a sense of not only how interactions between students and academics can lead to the development of shared understanding but also of how they can completely miss each other in the teaching–learning interactions because they are focused on different objects, which lead to different types of outcomes.

Situating teaching–learning environments in teaching–learning interactions

If teaching–learning environments are defined as the interacting activity systems of students and academics, then how are they situated or produced in particular teaching–learning interactions? As I have already discussed, Engeström (1987) is clear that generating activity systems is an empirical matter. The researcher comes to understand the activity system from the point of view of the agents involved and attempts to delineate a systematic view of the different aspects of the activity system. My approach to examining how teaching–learning environments are produced in particular teaching–learning interactions is to generate a generic model of the interacting activity systems of academics and students in higher education by drawing on existing research into teaching–learning processes in higher education. Clearly this is somewhat of a compromise, as the focus of Activity Theory is to generate an understanding of how local activity systems play out and interact in particular settings. However, this is a compromise that is intended to give a sense of the potential of Activity Theory to illuminate future analyses of the relations between teaching–learning environments and teaching–learning interactions.

Figure 4.3 gives a more developed sketch of the way in which the relations between teaching–learning environments and teaching–learning interactions can be conceived of in terms of the interacting activity systems of students and academics. This figure highlights the ways in which the teaching–learning environment is itself the product of structural–agentic processes because each node of the activity system is seen to be the ongoing product of other activity systems (see Russell and Yañez 2002 for an exploration of the different interlinking activity systems in which students are involved when studying in higher education).

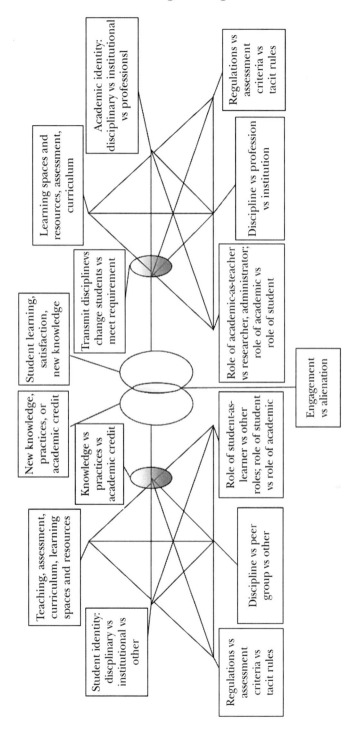

Figure 4.3: A further developed sketch of teaching–learning environments as the interacting activity systems of students and academics.

(Based on Engeström 2001, adapted and reprinted with the permission of the publisher: Taylor & Francis Ltd, www.tandf.co.uk/journals/titles/13639080.asp)

The subject of the student's activity is his or her identity in relation to this programme of study. This could be an identity as a novice member of their discipline or profession, as a member of the institution in which he or she is studying, or an identity from another activity system (see Solomon 2007; Warin and Dempster 2007). This is the product of their previous experiences both inside and outside of educational settings. There are tensions within this node of the activity system in terms of the tensions between the student's different identities as well as how the student's identity within the teaching–learning environment relates to their other identities in their wider lives. Russell and Yañez (2002) draw on the contradictions between the different activity systems in which students are engaged in order to show how they produce tensions in students' engagement in their studies.

Similarly, the subject of the academic's activity is their identity in relation to the element of the programme they are teaching. This could be an identity as a member of their discipline or profession, or as a member of their department or the wider university, or perhaps their identity as an intellectual (Clegg 2008a). This identity is again the product of their previous experiences both within educational and other activity systems, including engagement in their disciplines or professions (Shreeve 2008) and in professional development activities (Fanghanel 2004). The tensions within this node of the activity system are likely to be related to both the tensions between these identities and their identities within other activity systems (see Shreeve 2008 for an examination of the relations between the activity systems of Art and Design academics' teaching and professional practice, and Chapter 5 for a further discussion of these issues from the perspective of Symbolic Interactionism). It is worth noting that such a view addresses the common criticism that an Approaches to Learning and Teaching perspective focuses on disembodied 'teachers' and 'learners' (for example, see Ashwin 2008).

The student's primary object in the activity system can be focused on developing his or her disciplinary or professional knowledge and/or practices or on gaining academic credit (for example, see Marton *et al.* 1997). These objects are again the outcomes of previous activity systems, particularly previous educational experiences (for example, see O'Donnell and Tobbell 2007) and could be transformed into different kinds of outcomes: the development of new knowledge or practices or academic credit, although this knowledge and practices may not be those that were intended by those designing and teaching the programme. In their study of potential applicants to higher education, Hernandez-Martinez *et al.* (2008) give a good sense of the different objects that students can have in their learning of Mathematics.

The academic's object in the activity system can be focused on transmitting disciplinary or professional knowledge, on changing their students, or simply on meeting their institutional requirements in terms of the number of hours they will teach, which will be related to their prior experiences of teaching (for example, see Prosser and Trigwell 1999). These objects can be transformed into different kinds of outcomes for the academic: such as satisfaction or frustration with the quality of student learning or the development of new knowledge for the academic (for example, see Trigwell and Shale 2004).

While it is possible that the mediating artefacts within the two interacting activities might be very similar, the relations of students and academics to processes through which these are produced and situated in the teaching–learning environment are likely to be different. Some mediating artefacts, such as particular learning activities for students, may be designed by academics. Virtual and physical teaching–learning spaces are likely to be produced through institutional processes, with academics playing a role in configuring these for use in particular teaching–learning environments. Equally, other learning resources such as books or articles will be selected by academics as appropriate for supporting what they perceive as students' objects in the teaching–learning environment. While students may also introduce their own mediating artefacts into the teaching–learning environment, these are likely to have a less formal status. As well as having different relations to the production of mediating artefacts, students and academics are also likely to use them in different ways. Thus while the academic might use learning spaces, resources, assessment and the curriculum as mediating artefacts through which to meet their object of transmitting knowledge or changing students, for students these mediating artefacts are about their development of knowledge or completion of assessment tasks for academic credit (see Nespor 1994, 2007 for discussions of the way in which different ways of constituting space and time can impact on students' activities).

In a similar way, while the rules governing the academic and student might have similar sources in terms of institutional regulations, the assessment criteria and the tacit rules of teaching–learning interactions, the relation that students and academics have to the production of these rules is likely to be different, and the way in which these rules relate to their activity will be different because of their different roles on the programme and their different objects and identities. There can be tensions between these rules, for example an assessment criterion based on contributions to discussions but a tacit rule among students and academics that student contributions are not really welcome in teaching–learning interactions.

The student's community is related to who they see themselves as a subject and what they see as the object of their activity. For example, if they see themselves as fledging members of a discipline or profession, then their community could be others who are learning to be members of that community. Equally, if they are focused on gaining qualifications in order to develop themselves personally, then the community might be related to a familial group. Hernandez-Martinez *et al.* (2008) give a strong sense of how, even within apparently the same community such as the family, there can be differences in the ways in which these communities support the activity, which are related to, and inform, differences in the object of the activity system. Similarly, the academic's community is related to how they see themselves as a subject within their activity system, thus the community could be their discipline or profession or their institution. These communities are the outcomes of the interactions of other activity systems and enter into the activity system based on how they relate to other nodes.

Finally, the division of labour for students and academics has two elements to it. First, there is the relation between their role in this activity system and their other roles within and beyond higher education. For students, this could include how their role as a student-as-learner is related to their roles in other aspects of their lives both inside and outside of higher education. For example, if they are engaged in paid work and/or have caring responsibilities, this may reduce the time they have available for engaging in the activity system related to their higher education studies (see Callendar 2008). Similarly for academics, this aspect of the division of labour will be focused on how their role as academic-as–teacher relates to their particular status as a teacher, their other professional roles such as researcher and administrator, and their lives outside of higher education. Second, the division of labour focuses upon the relations between the different roles of student-as-learner, academic-as-teacher, and support staff within the teaching–learning environment. Each of these aspects of the division of labour is the outcome of other activity systems of the student, the academic and institutional processes.

In this way, Activity Theory highlights the ways in which different aspects of teaching–learning environments are produced and situated within teaching–learning interactions. In doing so, it emphasizes the ways in which students and academics are an integral part of teaching–learning environments rather than suggesting that teaching–learning environments are constituted before they come into relation to it. It also emphasizes that, rather than being fixed, teaching–learning environments change over time as the constituent parts of the activity systems of students and academics change due to their shifting relationships with other activity systems.

Characterizing teaching–learning interactions in terms of interacting activity systems

In thinking about how to characterize the teaching–learning interaction in terms of interacting activity systems, my focus moves from examining the relations between the interacting activity systems and other activity systems to examining the relations within the interacting activity systems of the student and academic. There are three aspects to this. First the relations between the different nodes of the activity systems generate students' and academics' initial experiences of the teaching–learning interaction; second over the course of the interaction, the objects of students and academics interact; and third, this interaction impacts on the activity systems of students and academics.

First, the teaching–learning interaction is initially generated through the relations between the different nodes of the activity systems. These relations can be considered in terms of the different triangles within the activity system; for example, the relations between students' identity, mediating artefacts, and the rules of the activity system. The Approaches to Learning and Teaching perspective gives a good sense of the different parts of the activity systems from the perspective of academics and students. Thus it is quite possible to relate the scales of the Experiences of Teaching–Learning Questionnaire (ETLQ)[1] (see Entwistle *et al.* 2003; Hounsell and Hounsell 2007) to different nodes of the student's activity systems, and the scales in Ramsden *et al.* (2007) to the different nodes of the academic's activity systems. However, it is important to recognize that as these inventories are based on students' and academics' perceptions, they always involve the consideration of the relation of the 'subject' node to the other nodes of the activity system. Activity Theory supports a wider examination of, for example, the relations between the rules, community and division of labour of the academic's activity system. These relations raise questions such as whether there are contradictions between what is expected of an academic-as-teacher in terms of institutional rules, the norms of their disciplinary community and the competing demands of their different professional roles.

Second, as the student and academic engage together, the objects of their activity systems interact. In Figure 4.3, the teaching–learning interaction is represented by the shaded overlap between the transformed outcome of the student and academic. I have drawn on Sarah Mann's work (Mann 2001, 2005; see also Case 2008) to suggest that, for both the student and academic, this could lead to a sense of engagement or alienation: engagement where there is a sense of a shared purpose, alienation where the activity systems of the student and academic appear to be directed at incompatible objects.

Third, this interaction between the activity systems of students and academics has the potential to feed back into the ongoing development of their activity systems, whether this be through altering their 'object', changing their sense of themselves as a 'subject', or changing their relation to another node of the activity system. Again it is important to think about the relations within and between the interacting activity systems as dynamic and shifting rather than as static and fixed.

In this way the teaching–learning interaction is characterized in terms of the interactions between the activity systems of the student and academic. This provides a sense of how the student and academic can have an ongoing and changing impact on each other's activity systems depending on what happens within the teaching–learning interaction.

The possibilities of an Activity Theory analysis of the relations between teaching–learning environments and teaching–learning interactions

I have identified a number of possibilities of adopting an Activity Theory approach to analysing the relations between teaching–learning environments and teaching–learning interactions. First, it offers a much more flexible definition of the teaching–learning environment because what is considered part of the teaching–learning environment is dependent on the activity systems of students and academics. This gives more space for the empirical world to have a role in defining what is constituted as the teaching–learning environment. Second, it highlights the processes through which the teaching–learning environment is itself the ongoing product of other activity systems, thus the teaching–learning environment can shift over time and the relations between its different aspects are seen as dynamic and shifting, a sense that is reinforced by the focus on the impact of contradictions within and between activity systems (for example, see Engeström 1987; Edwards 2005b). Finally, it provides a characterization of teaching–learning interactions in terms of teaching–learning environments through presenting these in terms of the interacting activity systems of students and academics.

The tensions in an Activity Theory analysis of the relations between teaching–learning environments and teaching–learning interactions

So far in this chapter, I have argued that conceptualizing teaching–learning environments in terms of interacting activity systems can help to address the shortcomings with the Approaches to Learning and Teaching perspective that I initially outlined in Chapter 3. I have argued that it helps to foreground the ways in which teaching–learning environments are situated in teaching–learning interactions and how teaching–learning interactions can be characterized in terms of teaching–learning environments.

I now want to focus on the tensions in adopting an Activity Theory perspective to analyse the relations between teaching–learning environments and teaching–learning interactions. I examine three tensions: whether Activity Theory is looked at from the perspective of an individual or collective subject; the categorization of the different nodes of the activity system; and the idea of the systematic view of activity systems.

The first tension is whether the interacting activity systems are those of individual students and academics or whether they are the collective activity systems of students and academics engaging within particular teaching–learning interactions. In discussing Figure 4.3, I focused on a generic individual student, but it was not clear whether this was an activity system for all students in a particular interaction or whether each student was part of a different activity system. There is a similar ambiguity in Engeström's research. When Engeström (1987, see Table 3.2) distinguishes goal-orientated action from an activity, one of the key differences is that goal-orientated actions are undertaken by individual subjects, while activity is undertaken by a collective subject. Similarly, when shifting from the action system to the activity system involved in writing an academic paper (Engeström 1999a, pp. 30-1), the subject shifts from 'me as an individual' to 'diverse group of scholars'. However, in much of Engeström's research the 'subject' element of an activity system is denoted by a role such as 'general practitioner', 'hospital practitioner', 'parent' (see for example, Engeström 1994, 2000, 2001) and the subsequent analyses suggest that these relate to individual agents.

Davydov (1999) argues that this is one of the major unsolved problems of Activity Theory. The problem is this. If Activity Theory focuses on the activity systems of individuals it loses its sense of a collective engagement in tasks situated within a common community, division of labour and subject to the same rules. It instead becomes focused on individual perceptions and implies that if, for example, students perceive the same teaching–learning interaction differently, then they are engaged in different activities. In this way, an Activity Theory perspective loses its potential to account for the aspects of the activity system beyond the perceptions of students and academics. However, if it focuses, for example, on collective activity systems of students, then it is not clear how students with different objects can be incorporated into the same activity system. This is because unless they are focused on the same object of activity, it is not clear that they are part of the same activity system in any meaningful sense. One potential resolution of this tension might be to group students according to the objects of their activity, as Engeström (1995) appears to do with medical practitioners. However, this would need to be done with care so that these groupings did not become static and a sense of how the different objects of activity impacted on each other was still maintained. This would involve keeping a close focus on the relations between an Activity Theory perspective and the empirical data generated to examine the relations between teaching–learning environments and teaching–learning interactions.

The second tension is related to the six categories that are seen to make up activity systems. It is clear that different researchers attach different meanings to the different nodes of the activity system. For example, in relation to the 'community' element of the activity systems, within studies related to learners within education the 'community' is sometimes seen as other members of the class or student group (Havnes 2004; Engeström 1990), sometimes the wider institution or discipline (Coupland and Crawford 2002; Barab *et al.* 2002; Scanlon and Isroff 2005) sometimes the world beyond the institution (Mwanza and Engeström 2005). While this could be related to differences in the activity systems under consideration, often it seems to be based on the assumptions of the researchers. However, the greater problem is that it is clear that the different categories are not mutually exclusive. I have already discussed the ways in which assessment could be positioned in different ways in different activity systems but it is also not always clear that within a single activity system it can be assigned to one node. For example, the same assessment task could be seen by the same student as being part of the rules governing their activity, a mediating artefact through which they gain understanding, as well as an outcome they achieve. A response to this is to argue that the same piece of assessment can embody different parts of the activity system, but this raises the issue of at what level the activity system is seen to exist; that is, the ontological status of activity systems.

There are two positions that can be taken as to the ontological status of the activity systems. They can either be argued to exist 'out there' in the real world or they can be seen as a heuristic device that the researcher uses to simplify the real world in order to engage with it. Generally, Engeström is clear that it is a framework (for example, see

Engeström 2000), which is reflected in his discussions of the development of the theory (for example, Engeström 2001), and this is certainly what other researchers drawing on Engeström's work seem to do. For example, Barab *et al.* (2002) use the different parts of the activity system as categories for analysing their data. Such an approach to activity systems is consistent with the approach to ontology and epistemology outlined in Chapter 2.

The problem with this is that if Activity Theory is being used to simplify the real world, then a lack of clarity in relation to which aspects of the empirical world can be categorized under particular aspects of the model suggest that this is a limitation of Activity Theory as both a heuristic and an explanatory device. This is because rather than helping the development of an understanding of the complex social world, it introduces confusion about how to interpret aspects of that world. A way of resolving this tension would be not to limit a consideration of Activity Theory to the six categories that Engeström (1987) develops from Leont'ev (1978) but rather to examine other potential nodes of the activity system. Thus in researching activity systems one could consider how subjects use mediating tools to try to achieve their objects, which are transformed into outcomes, but then not assume that rules, the division of labour and community, are the only, or even among, the processes that structure this activity. In a way, this is the approach that has been taken by other Cultural–Historical Activity Theorists (for example, see Edwards 2005a and Hernandez-Martinez *et al.* 2008). This tension again highlights the importance of carefully examining the relations between perspectives used to conceptualize teaching–learning interactions and empirical data generated relating to these interactions.

The third tension is in relation to the participant's view and the systematic view of the activity system. In order to be consistent it is clear that rather than the analyst providing a systematic view of the activity systems they are investigating, they rather provide a view of these activity systems from their activity systems as researchers. This means that the 'systematic' view would be more modestly called the 'researchers' view' of the activity system. This would have the advantage of explicitly recognizing that the researcher is engaged in a different activity system, which is focused on a different object, from those they research. Thus while students and academics are focused on teaching–learning processes, the analyst is focused on research activities.[2] Such an approach would increase the reflexivity of the research, an issue to which I return in Chapter 8. As with the other two tensions, this again suggests the need to think about how the conceptual perspective adopted to analyse teaching–learning interactions influences the way in which the empirical world is approached.

Conclusion

In this chapter, I have explored how adopting an Activity Systems perspective to analyse the relations between teaching–learning environments and teaching–learning interactions addresses the limitations of an Approaches to Learning and Teaching approach to analysing these relations. I have also identified a number of tensions in drawing on an Activity Theory approach to analysing these relations. I argued that the impact of these tensions can be minimized by keeping a clear focus on the relations between Activity Theory as a conceptual approach and empirical data that is generated to explore teaching–learning interactions in higher education. Even given these tensions, an Activity Theory perspective appears to have potential in supporting an analysis of the relations between teaching–learning environments and teaching–learning interactions in higher education.

Notes

1   A similar argument could be made based on the scales in Ramsden's (1991) Course Experience Questionnaire.
2   I thank Ann Kendrick for suggesting this point.

Chapter 5

Analysing the relations between student and academic identities and teaching–learning interactions

Introduction

In this chapter, I explore Symbolic Interactionism as a way of analysing the relations between student and academic identities and teaching–learning interactions in higher education. I first examine my reasons for focusing on Symbolic Interactionism before introducing it as an approach to analysing the relations between student and academic identities and teaching–learning interactions in higher education. I explore how it can give a sense of both how student and academic identities are produced within teaching–learning interactions and how teaching–learning interactions can be conceptualized in terms of the relations between student and academic identities. Finally, I explore the possibilities and tensions of adopting a Symbolic Interactionist approach to analysing the relations between student and academic identities and teaching–learning interactions in higher education.

Why use Symbolic Interactionism to analyse the relations between student and academic identities and teaching–learning interactions?

In Chapter 3, I argued that while an Academic Literacies approach to analysing the relations between student and academic identities and teaching–learning interactions foregrounds how students' and academics' identities are produced in relation to teaching–learning interactions, it does not give a sense of how to conceptualize teaching–learning interactions in terms of the relations between the identities of students and academics. In this chapter, I argue that Symbolic Interactionism provides a useful framework with which to analyse the relations between student and academic identities and teaching–learning interactions.

Before I examine Symbolic Interactionism in more detail, it is necessary to say something about drawing on it in a project that is partly aimed at developing accounts of the interplay between structure and agency in teaching–learning interactions. This is because it is common to criticize Symbolic Interactionism for merely focusing on people's experiences without considering how these experiences are structured by wider forces. For example, some argue that Symbolic Interactionism has an astructural bias (see Denzin 1992 for a summary of such criticisms) or an ahistorical bias which assumes a simplistic pluralist macro theory as a backdrop to interactions (see Hammersley 1980).

My response to such criticisms is to argue that while this may be a problem with particular Symbolic Interactionism studies, it is not an inherent problem with Symbolic Interactionism (see Law 1994 for a similar argument). Symbolic Interactionism sees society as an emergent phenomenon, and Mead (1934), whose work provided a major strand in the development of Symbolic Interactionism, saw the mind, self and society as different aspects of the same *processes* (see Maines 2001; Atkinson and Housley 2003). The gaps between these different aspects are vital because they provide spaces for contingency, spaces in which people could have acted otherwise and things could have developed differently (McCall and Becker 1990).

Symbolic Interactionism

A number of recent books have argued that the influence of Symbolic Interactionism on research in the social sciences has been obscured. Atkinson and Housley (2003) in their subtitle refer to 'sociological amnesia', while Maines (2001, p. 16) identifies 'unaware interactionists'. In different ways, both of these books argue that many are working within the Symbolic Interactionism tradition without being aware of it.

As a research approach, Symbolic Interactionism is based on the US pragmatism of, among others, Dewey and Mead (see Denzin 1992). It should be noted that Symbolic Interactionism cannot be seen as a single approach. A number of different versions of Symbolic Interactionism developed in the US (see Denzin 1992; Holstein and Gubrium 2000) and in the UK (see Atkinson and Housley 2003). However, as Denzin (1992) argues, its canonical form can be seen in the work of

Blumer (1969). Blumer (1969, p. 50) argues that Symbolic Interactionism can be seen as resting on four assumptions:

1. Human beings act towards things on the basis of the meanings that the things have for them.
2. The meanings of things arise out of the process of social interaction.
3. These meanings are modified through an interpretative process which involves self-reflective individuals symbolically interacting with one another.
4. The complex interlinkages of acts that constitute institutions are moving, not static, affairs.

Thus the 'symbolic' aspect of Symbolic Interactionism stresses the ways in which people ascribe meanings to the actions of others and how this informs their choices about how to act. It is in this way that people both 'fit' their actions together in social situations and form their own actions. The interactionism element stresses that:

> Both such joint activity and individual conduct are formed *in* and *through* this ongoing process; they are not the mere expressions or products of what people bring to their interactions or of conditions antecedent to their interaction. (Blumer 1969, p. 10, emphasis in the original)

This approach has a number of implications for conducting research. First, there is a need to focus on the *processes* through which people make sense of and engage collectively in social interactions rather than simply looking for what they bring to the situation, whether this is their practices or perceptions of social situations. Second, it suggests that developing an understanding of the meanings that actors ascribe to these ongoing interactions is essential. As Blumer (1969) argues, this means that researchers need to be careful in the way in which they approach understanding the social world. Such understanding needs to be based on data about the meanings that actors continually develop in social interactions. Thus Bulmer (1969, pp. 147–8) argues against researchers approaching the social world with 'definitive concepts' that tell them what is where before they examine it, and rather that they draw on 'sensitizing concepts' which 'gives the user a general sense of reference and guidance . . . [and] . . . merely suggest directions along which to look'.

None of this should be taken to imply that people have perfect knowledge of what they do in social interactions; Blumer (1969) is clear that there are layers of such interactions that are hidden to the participants. Rather it is to imply that the way in which participants continually and collectively make meanings in and through social interactions is a crucial element in understanding the social world.

Conceptualizing student and academic identities from a Symbolic Interactionist perspective

Given its focus on the contingency of the outcomes of interactions, it is perhaps not surprising that interactionist texts tend not to offer definitions of identity but rather offer what could be seen as 'sensitizing concepts' for thinking about how such identities are formed (for example, see Strauss 1969 and Williams 2000).

I want to highlight five aspects of a Symbolic Interactionist view of identity. First, as the previous section suggests, within a Symbolic Interactionism perspective, the focus on identity is on how identities are developed and ascribed in interactions with others. As Williams (2000) argues, this means that issues of identity make sense in a local context because they arise and are dealt with in the socially organized practices of everyday life. This means that people are seen as developing different identities in relation to different aspects of their lives. Thus Symbolic Interactionism does not involve the conceptualization of an essential identity.

Second, people are not seen as creating new identities in every social interaction. Rather, people enter into particular types of interactions with established identities and ways of dealing with other participants (Bulmer 1969; Goffman[1] 1983). Even if it is a new situation, such as entering higher education, they will draw on schemes of interpretation that they have already developed in other situations that they see as comparable to the current situation. Thus it is vital to examine the historical links between situations from the perspectives of particular actors.

Third, part of what defines a type of situation is its institutional location. Thus Goffman emphasizes the normative requirements and local institutional arrangements that impact on the dynamic and socially situated formation of identity (see Goffman 1959, 1961, 1963). Within such institutional settings people develop 'careers' (Goffman 1961, 1963; Becker 1963), which reflect both people's felt identity within a particular context as well as their institutional position, be it in a mental hospital (see Goffman 1961), a primary school (see Pollard and Filer 1999a,b), or in relation to a particular aspect of their lives such as 'learning' (Bloomer 1997, 2001 and Bloomer and Hodkinson 1997, 1999, 2000) or forms of 'deviance' (Becker 1963).

Fourth, within a particular institution, people can have different aspects to their careers. Thus in relation to higher education, the focus could be on people's overall careers as 'academics' (as is common in non-symbolic interactionist literature in higher education, see Henkel 2000; Harris 2005; Archer 2008a,b; Clegg 2008a,b; Taylor 2008) or 'students' (see Kaufman and Feldman 2004; Ahearn *et al.* 2008), or their different careers within the institution as, for example, 'researchers' and 'teachers' or 'learners' and 'members of a wider university'. I choose the latter approach because these careers are likely to have different types of interactions associated with them and, while some might see clear relations between their different careers within an institution, their relation is contingent, and viewing them as separate careers allows a focus on the relations between them.

Fifth, as well as careers, people have a sense of their personal identity, of who they are outside of their institutional roles (Goffman 1963; Williams 2000). Personal identities are equally dynamic and develop over time. Aspects of personal identities can be important in informing how people approach particular careers.

To summarize, interactions are seen to take place in particular institutional settings. Within an interaction, aspects of different careers and different aspects of a personal identity can be foregrounded at different times. For example, within a teaching–learning interaction an academic's career as a 'teacher', a 'researcher' or their personal identity as a woman might be foregrounded over the course of the interaction. Together these points highlight two aspects of identity. First, there is identity as an outcome, the careers that people have developed up to a particular moment within a particular institutional setting. Second, there is identity as performed in a particular interaction. This draws on people's institutional careers but is contingent of what occurs within a particular interaction.

In the following sections I draw on the notion of students' learning, and academics' teaching, careers to examine how a Symbolic Interactionism approach can be used to analyse the relations between student and academic identities and teaching–learning interactions. In examining these relations, I refer to educational research in higher education that has drawn on a Symbolic Interactionism perspective. However, apart from the classic Symbolic Interactionism studies from the 1960s (for example, see Becker *et al.* 1961, 1968 and Olesen and Whittaker 1968), there is not a great amount of empirical research to draw upon. Thus I also draw on Symbolic Interactionism informed research in schools and further education, as well as non-Symbolic Interactionism informed research within higher education, in order to inform and illustrate my argument for how a Symbolic Interactionism approach can inform an understanding of the relations between academic and student identities and teaching–learning interactions in higher education. It is important to be clear that, in relation to the non-Symbolic Interactionist research, I reinterpret its outcomes and arguments in terms of students' learning careers and academics' teaching careers, but these were not the terms used in the original research.

Situating student and academic identities in teaching–learning interactions

In examining how academics' and students' identities are situated in teaching-interactions, I argue that they are situated in the form of their respective teaching and learning careers up to a particular moment in time. I argue that these forms are the product of the relations between their personal identities, their other institutional careers, and the previous histories of their teaching and learning careers. This focus is similar to Pollard and Filer's examination of pupils' careers in school education (Pollard with Filer 1996; Pollard and Filer 1999a,b; Filer and Pollard 2000; Pollard and Filer 2007; Pollard 2007). For example, Pollard and Filer (1999a) argued that such careers were made up of patterns of previous outcomes of learning, interactions and experiences in the wider context of the school; patterns of strategic ways of coping and acting in these contexts; and the students' evolving sense of themselves within these contexts. Similarly Symbolic Interactionism informed research in British schools in the 1980s (see for example, Hargreaves 1972; Woods 1980a,b, 1983, 1996; Pollard 1982, 1985; Delamont 1983) gave a strong sense of how pupils and teachers develop their learning and teaching careers in relation to the pupil and teacher cultures of the school (see Atkinson and Housley 2003, Chapter 4, for a recent summary and appraisal).

In their work with the careers of school pupils, Pollard and Filer (2007) give a clear sense of how pupils' personal identities impacted on the development of their learning careers. They argue that social class and gender impact on the learning careers that pupils developed within schools and on their expectations for the future. Similarly, in their work on the learning careers of further education students, Bloomer and Hodkinson (1997, 1999, 2000) argued that students' gender, class and their lives outside of college had an impact on the paths of their learning careers (see also Bloomer 1997; Hodkinson and Bloomer 2000). In research in higher education, from perspectives other than Symbolic Interactionism, similar accounts have been developed. Thus students from different social classes, ethnic groups, genders and ages may draw on different resources when engaging in higher education (see for example, Archer and Leathwood 2003; Power *et al.* 2003; Reay 2003; Bufton 2006; Haggis 2006). Part of these factors are students' previous experiences in education (Forsyth and Furlong 2003; Gorard *et al.* 2007) and the time they have available to develop their careers as students in higher education, given the other calls on their time (for example, see Metcalf 2003; Christie *et al.* 2005; Moreau and Leathwood 2006; and Callender 2008 on the impact of paid work on students' experiences of higher education).

It is important to emphasize that such factors are not seen as operating in a deterministic or uniform manner. As Archer and Leathwood (2003) argue, there is no single working-class identity and, indeed, no single middle-class identity (see Power *et al.* 2003). Rather, these aspects of students' personal identities inform how they understand and engage with the development of their learning careers in higher education. Equally, students' other institutional careers within higher education can play a role in shaping their learning careers. For example, Solomon (2007) explores the relations between students'

identities in Mathematics and their other identities in higher education.

Compared to students' learning careers, academics' teaching careers
generally develop over a much longer timeframe. For this reason, it may
be that their other institutional careers have more of an impact than for
students. Thus academics' careers as 'researchers' and 'administrators'
can have an impact on their teaching careers both in the way in which
they perceive their teaching career and the time they have available for
the development of each of these careers (see Henkel 2000; Sikes 2006;
Deem and Lucas 2007). Equally, their personal identities in terms of
their social class, gender and race can impact on the development of
their teaching careers (for example, see Mizra 1995; Rassool 1995;
Anderson and Williams 2001; Bhopal 2002; Hey 2003; Reay 2004; Deem
and Lucas 2007; Clegg 2008b).

So far I have argued that students' and academics' personal identities and other institutional careers have an impact on the development
of their respective learning and teaching careers. However, these
learning and teaching careers also have a history that impacts on their
subsequent development. The classic Symbolic Interactionism studies
of the 1960s give a sense of how students' learning careers develop over
time in higher education. Becker *et al.* (1961, 1968) argue that
students' initial general and fairly idealistic perspectives of how they
will engage with higher education change to focus on giving their
teachers 'what they want' in the case of the medical students in Becker
et al. (1961), and focusing on gaining a 'good grade' in the case of
students in Becker *et al.* (1968). For academics there is less literature
that gives a sense of how their careers as teachers develop over time.
However, Deem and Lucas (2007) argue that the career histories of
academics within education departments play a role in shaping their
orientation to both teaching and research. Equally, McLean (2006)
argues that those at the start of their teaching careers are 'vulnerable'
both inside and outside of teaching–learning interactions. Given the
way in which teaching and learning careers are seen to solidify over
time in a particular institution, it is not surprising that research has
focused on the way in which entering a new educational institution has
an impact on academics' (Trowler and Knight 2000) and students'
(Cassidy and Trew 2001; O'Donnell and Tobbell 2007; Warin and
Dempster 2007) respective careers.

The ways in which these careers develop over time is also related to the teaching–learning environments and disciplinary and institutional settings in which they take shape. The teaching–learning environment can inform the development of students' learning and academics' teaching careers. For example, research from an Academic Literacies perspective can be interpreted as examining how particular writing and reading tasks can shape students' learning careers (Clark and Ivanič 1997; Ivanič 1998; Mann 2000; Lillis 2001; Paxton 2003). Similarly, Approaches to Learning and Teaching research can be interpreted as giving a sense of how academics can interpret their teaching role differently depending on their perceptions of the teaching–learning environment (for example, see Prosser and Trigwell 1997).

The disciplinary settings of students' learning careers, and academics' teaching careers, can impact on the development of these careers. There is some evidence that different disciplines involve quite different career paths for students over their time in higher education. For example, in his Actor-Network informed studies, Nespor (1994, 2007) gives a clear sense of how differences in the way time and space are constituted in physics, management and sociology lead students to have very different kinds of learning careers within these disciplines. In relation to academics, studies from a number of perspectives argue that academics' disciplinary identities play a key role in shaping their teaching identities (Henkel 2000; Pickering 2006; Abbas and McLean 2007b, Windberg 2008) although in some contexts these are argued to be less significant (Sikes 2006; Clegg 2008a). It is also important to recognize that, depending on the relations between their different institutional careers and personal identities, different academics can experience the same disciplines in different ways and that these experiences can change over time (for example, see Brew 2008).

The institutional setting of students' learning careers, and academics' teaching careers, may also impact on their development. For example, how the role of student is seen can differ institutionally, for example the extent to which students are seen as 'consumers' (Naidoo and Jamieson 2006), and the institutional approach that is taken to the development of independent learners (Leathwood and O'Connell 2003; Leathwood 2006; Smith 2007). For academics, different institutions position the teaching, research and administrative careers of academics in different ways, which offer different opportunities and constraints for the development of teaching careers (Henkel 2000, 2005; Harris 2005; Lucas 2006, 2007; Sikes 2006). Similarly, different opportunities and constraints are offered by different institutions' demands in terms of the programmes that are taught (James 2007) and the forms of support for developing academics' teaching careers (Gosling 2008). As with all of the factors outlined above, the institutional settings do not act in a deterministic way; rather, depending on the relations between their different institutional careers and personal identities, different academics can respond to the same institutional setting in different ways (for example, see Trowler 1998; Fanghanel 2007).

The processes described above give a sense of how students' and academics' identities are situated in teaching–learning interactions in the form of their respective learning and teaching careers at a particular moment in time. They show how these careers are shaped by the relations between their personal identities, their other institutional careers and the settings in which they are developed. The development of these careers up to a particular point in time informs how students and academics understand themselves as 'learners' and 'teachers' in particular teaching–learning interactions. It is to how these identities play out in relation to each other in particular interactions that I now turn.

Characterizing teaching–learning interactions in terms of the relation between student and academic identities

In the previous section, I foregrounded student and academic identities through examining the development of their learning and teaching careers. In this section I foreground the teaching–learning interaction and examine how teaching–learning interactions can be characterized in terms of the identities of students and academics. In examining this, I again focus on students' and academics' personal identities, the teaching–learning environment, and the disciplinary and institutional setting of the interaction. Again, I am not claiming that these are the only processes that impact on the relations between student and academic identities but rather that these are processes that are generally considered important in literature on teaching–learning processes in higher education. My argument is that these processes potentially contain different identity positions for academics and students that they can take up in relation to each other over the course of teaching–learning interactions.

As I argued in the introductory chapter, higher education research has not focused on the dynamic ways in which teaching–learning interactions shift and change over time. Perhaps surprisingly, the same is true of much Symbolic Interactionism research into higher education. Generally the classic Symbolic Interactionism studies (Becker *et al.* 1961, 1968) tend to focus on the development of students' perspectives in higher education rather than on the interplay between academics' and students' identities within particular interactions. In line with Mead (1934, pp. 152–6), students' relationships with academics were treated as the relationship with a 'generalized other'. While Olesen and Whittaker's (1968) study of nursing does examine students' collective reaction to particular academics, the focus is on common ways in which students deal with these academics rather than on the different ways in which identities interact. Part of the reason for this is undoubtedly due to the perceived homogeneity of students in these studies. Indeed Delamont and Atkinson (1995) argue that the focus on the homogeneity of students and the domination of institutional processes were major factors in Symbolic Interactionism studies becoming less popular. With both student (see Jary and Jones 2006; Archer 2006; Crozier *et al.* 2008), and academics (Harris 2005; Barnett and Di Napoli 2008; Clegg 2008b) drawn from more diverse backgrounds, such assumptions are certainly unsustainable now.

The more recent Symbolic Interactionist studies in further education (Bloomer 1997, 2001 and Bloomer and Hodkinson 1997, 1999, 2000) and compulsory education (Pollard with Filer 1996; Pollard and Filer 1999a,b; Filer and Pollard 2000; Pollard and Filer 2007; Pollard 2007) cited earlier, again foreground the development of students' or pupils' careers rather than the interplay of identities within particular interactions. Similarly non-Symbolic Interactionist research into teaching–learning interactions in problem-based learning (for example, see Koschmann *et al.* 2000; Duek 2000) and on-line learning (for example, see Dawson 2006) in higher education foreground the activity of academics or students and not the way in which their identities relate to each other over the course of particular interactions. This is unfortunate because it tends to obscure the way in which the identity positions available for students and academics are intimately related.

As Strauss (1969, p. 55) argues about face-to-face interaction more generally:

> Face-to-face interaction is a fluid, moving, 'running' process; during its course the participants take successive stances vis-à-vis each other. Sometimes they fence, sometimes they move in rhythmic psychological ballet, but always they move through successive phases of position.

It is this sense of interactions that I am trying to capture in order to characterize teaching–learning interactions in terms of academic and student identities. To draw on the previous sections, I am arguing that in particular teaching–learning interactions there are many factors that contribute to the identity positions that students and academics move through in relation to each other. Thus in responding to each other, students and academics may perceive that different positions are available to them depending on their 'teaching' or 'learning' careers, their personal identities, the teaching–learning environment and the disciplinary and institutional settings of the interactions. Within a particular interaction these different aspects of identity can move into the foreground and into the background of students' and academics' experiences of the interaction, thus sometimes students' or academics' race or gender might feel central to interaction (for an example, see Bhopal 2002), but at other times disciplinary identities might come to the fore.

My argument is that these different processes are related to different relations between student and academic identities within teaching–learning interactions (see Chappell *et al.* 2003 for a similar analysis of adult education from a different perspective). Thus different 'learning' and 'teaching' careers of students and academics lead them to have particular senses of what it means to engage within a particular teaching–learning interaction (see Mann 2003 for a fascinating example of how different academics' and students' experiences of how these play out in a particular interaction can be). The teaching–learning environment can impact on the positions that students and academics take up in relation to each other (on the relations between their positions in seminars, see Fejes *et al.* 2005, and clinical settings, see Atkinson 1997). The disciplinary setting may also impact on the range of positions that students and academics can take up in relation to each other, perhaps through a sense of the appropriate relations between full, and student, members of a particular discipline or professional area (see for example, Solomon 2007). Finally, the institutional setting can impact on the identity positions that students and academics can adopt in relation to each other. One of the main ways this is done is through the organization of the spaces (whether physical or virtual) in which teaching–learning interactions take place (see Bourdieu *et al.* 1994; Nespor 1994, 2007; Jones *et al.* 2005; Bruce *et al.* 2007 for discussions of the way teaching–learning spaces can shape interactions).

There are three other points that are central to such a characterization of teaching–learning interactions in terms of student and academic identities. First, by focusing on the relations between the identity positions of students and academics, issues of power are brought to the fore. This is because there are usually differences in the power that are related to such positions. However, how power plays out in particular interactions is still contingent on how students and academics handle the interaction. Second, there is no claim here that academics and students necessarily make rational or explicit choices about the identity positions that they move through in relation to each other in particular interactions, often they are thrust upon them in the course of interaction rather than being the result of careful reflection (Sfard and Prusak 2004). Third, it is clear that some of the identity positions from the different settings may hold contradictory meanings for academics and students. For example, there may be conflicts between what course of action is implied by disciplinary and gender identities (see Thomas 1990 on the relations between gender and discipline identities in English and Physics, and Nespor 1994 on women's position in study group activities in Physics).

So characterizing teaching–learning interactions in terms of student and academic identities focuses on the shifting identity positions that students and academics take up in relation to each other over the course of an interaction. Thus the teaching–learning interaction is characterized in terms of the ways in which students and academics impact on the identity positions that each takes up in relation to the other.

The possibilities of a Symbolic Interactionist analysis of the relations between the student and academic identities and teaching–learning interactions

I have identified four possibilities of a Symbolic Interactionist approach to analysing the relations between student and academic identities and teaching–learning interactions. First, it gives a good sense of how student and academic identities become situated in the teaching–learning environment through the concept of students' learning and academics' teaching careers. This highlights the ways in which student and academic identities in teaching–learning interactions are related to their previous experiences in educational and other settings, as well as to their other careers within the institutional setting of the teaching–learning interaction. Second, it focuses on students' learning and academics' teaching careers as emergent rather than fixed. Thus they change over time and, while it gives a sense of how students' learning and academics' teaching careers are shaped by their personal identities, their other institutional careers, the teaching–learning environment, and disciplinary and institutional factors, these factors do not operate in a deterministic manner. Rather, they offer different resources that students and academics can draw upon, consciously or subconsciously, in different ways over the course of developing their careers. Third, it provides a way of conceptualizing teaching–learning interactions in terms of the interactions between student and academic identities that highlights the shifting identity positions that academics and students move through in relation to each other within particular interactions. Finally, it gives a sense of how different aspects of identity may be foregrounded over the course of a particular interaction. This view of identity is similar to Holstein and Gubrium's (2000) narrative view of the self in which the self is seen as continually under construction and constructed at the crossroads of institutional discourses, the interplay of discursive practice and dis-courses-in-practice. In doing so it provides a sense of the way in which student and academic identities relate to each other in particular teaching–learning interactions, which was a limitation of the Academic Literacies perspective.

The tensions in a Symbolic Interactionist analysis of the relations between student and academic identities and teaching–learning interactions

I identify three tensions in adopting a Symbolic Interactionist approach to analysing the relations between student and academic identities and teaching–learning interactions. First, there is a tension in the way in which different processes are seen to relate to the development of the learning and teaching careers of students and academics. To take social class as an example, there is a tension between how much it is seen as an individual or a collective experience. Focusing too much on the ways in which individuals can draw on their experiences of class in different ways seems to lose a focus on the collective elements of social class that are a vital part of how it is experienced, while focusing too much on the collective elements may give the impression that there are no differences in the experiences of those from the same position in terms of social class. This is not a tension that can be resolved but something that needs to be returned to and struggled with in examining the relations between students' and academics' personal identities and their learning and teaching careers.

Second, there is a tension between the way in which student learning, and academic teaching, careers are seen to the outcome of strategic planning or of unreflective reactions to the situations in which they find themselves. Brooks and Everett (2008b) suggest that there may be differences in the way in which different students plan their paths through higher education, with those with more privileged learning careers in terms of the status of their institution and academic success being *less* likely to form detailed plans for the future. There could be a range of reasons for this. Brooks and Everett (2008b) suggest it may be related to a sense of security about the future. However, it could also be, as Bourdieu *et al.* (1994) would suggest, related to the effortless fit between privileged students' learning careers and their institutional cultures, which means that there is no need to consciously think about where they are going (see Chapter 7 for further discussion of these ideas). Again, this is not a tension that can be resolved but a question to return to when drawing on empirical evidence to analyse the relations between student and academic identities and teaching–learning interactions.

Third, there is a tension between how much shared understanding is assumed in teaching–learning interactions between students and academics. In examining Strauss's (1969, p. 155) 'psychological ballet', there can be a tendency to assume that students and academics recognize the positions that each other is taking. Mann's (2003) analysis of a teaching–learning interaction in higher education suggests that these can be fraught with frustrating misunderstandings and miscommunications. Again, in analysing the relations between student and academic identities and teaching–learning interactions it is important not to assume that the participants have shared understandings of those interactions. This raises a methodological issue about how the data are generated in relation to teaching–learning interactions that I will explore in more detail in Chapter 8.

Conclusion

In this chapter I have argued that adopting a Symbolic Interactionist perspective to analysing the relations between student and academic identities and teaching–learning interactions provides both a sense of how these identities are situated in teaching–learning interactions and how teaching–learning interactions can be characterized in terms of academics' and students' identities. I also identified three tensions in adopting a Symbolic Interactionist approach to analysing these relations: the extent to which the individual or collective aspects of teaching and learning careers are focused on, the extent to which such careers are seen as the outcome of deliberate planning, and the extent to which it is assumed that there is shared understanding between student and academics in teaching–learning interactions.

In the next chapter I examine how the work of Basil Bernstein can be used in analysing the relations between disciplinary knowledge practices and teaching–learning interactions in higher education.

Note

1   While Goffman himself did not identify himself as a Symbolic Interactionist, most see his work as closely related to, or part of, Symbolic Interactionism (see for example, Denzin 1992; Charon 2001; Atkinson and Housley 2003).

Chapter 6

Analysing the relations between disciplinary knowledge practices and teaching–learning interactions

Introduction

In this chapter, I examine how the ideas of Basil Bernstein, as well as the development of his work by others, might offer a way of analysing the relations between disciplinary knowledge practices and teaching–learning interactions. I first outline my reasons for examining a Bernsteinian approach before outlining how it supports an analysis of the relations between disciplinary knowledge practices and teaching–learning interactions through the concept of the 'Pedagogic Device' (Bernstein 1990, 2000). I argue that the Pedagogic Device offers a way of both analysing how disciplinary knowledge practices are situated in teaching–learning interactions and a way of conceptualizing teaching–learning interactions in terms of disciplinary knowledge practices. Finally, I consider the possibilities and tensions of adopting a Bernsteinian approach to analysing the relations between disciplinary knowledge practices and teaching–learning interactions in higher education.

Why examine a Bernsteinian approach to analysing the relations between disciplinary knowledge practices and teaching–learning interactions?

In Chapter 3, I examined a Communities of Practice perspective as a way of analysing the relations between disciplinary knowledge practices and teaching–learning interactions. I argued that there were two problems with this approach. First, in relation to examining how disciplinary knowledge practices are situated in teaching–learning interactions, I argued that a Community of Practice perspective appears to assume that discipline-as-research is the same as discipline-as-curriculum. By this I mean that it assumes that the knowledge practices involved in research activities in a particular discipline are the same as the knowledge practices involved in the higher education curricula related to that discipline. Second, in order to offer a characterization of teaching–learning interactions in terms of disciplinary knowledge practices, it requires the assumption to be made that students and academics are members of the same disciplinary community of practice, that students are focused on becoming members of academics' disciplinary community.

The focus of Bernstein's (1990, 2000) research is on the 'voice' of pedagogic communication, on how knowledge, power and control come together in teaching–learning processes. From Bernstein's (1990, 2000) perspective, many education theories are focused on how discourses of education reproduce relations of social class, gender and racial inequality that are external to the discourse of education – what Bernstein (1990, 2000) calls 'pedagogic discourse'. This means that the pedagogic discourse is only seen as a 'carrier' of other discourses and is 'only a voice through which others speak' while its 'own voice is absent' (Bernstein 1990, p. 166). Rather than analysing *relations to* pedagogic communication, Bernstein's (1990, 2000) focus is on analysing *relations within* pedagogic communication by developing an understanding of the voice of pedagogic discourse.

There are two aspects of Bernstein's (1990, 2000) analysis of the voice of pedagogic discourse that appear to offer an alternative way of analysing the relations between disciplinary knowledge practices and teaching–learning interactions. First, he provides conceptual tools to analyse how disciplinary knowledge is produced and transformed into curriculum and, second, how curriculum and teaching–learning interactions potentially shape the consciousness of academics and students. As Arnot and Reay (2004, p. 137) argue, '[Bernstein's theory] is unique in formulating connections between the organization and structuring of knowledge, the means by which it is transmitted and the ways in which acquisition is experienced.'

This focus is related to Bernstein's (1990, 2000) explicit consideration of how micro and macro factors can be incorporated into an understanding of pedagogic communication. For example, in his consideration of the criteria he had for his theory, his first criterion focuses on how to relate interaction and structural aspects of the theory. He argues that 'macro-constraints must be made visible by the conceptual language, in their power to shape interactions. At the same time the potential of interactions to shape macro-constraints must be capable of being described' (Bernstein 2000, p. 91).

Thus Bernstein (1990, 2000) seeks to provide an explicit link between the macro processes of knowledge production and the micro processes of teaching–learning interactions.

Reading Bernstein

In examining how Bernstein's theory of the pedagogic device can offer an approach to analysing the relations between disciplinary knowledge practices and teaching–learning interactions, I focus mainly on the last two volumes of Bernstein's *Class, Codes and Control* series. This is for two reasons. First, the five volumes of this series represent an ongoing development of Bernstein's theory. Thus while each volume builds on its predecessor, the changes over time are significant, and each volume, to some extent, offers a reinterpretation of the theory. This is because an essential part of Bernstein's project was to develop a theory that was interrogated by empirical data and was developed and changed as a result of this interrogation (see Bernstein's 2000, pp. 125–6, consideration of the relation between theory and research). Second, it is in the later development of his theory, in volumes IV and V (Bernstein 1990 and 2000), that Bernstein explicitly develops the pedagogic device to link the micro-context of educational interactions and the macro-context of social and political structures.

One issue that faces all those who seek to explore the Bernsteinian approach in new contexts is the extent to which they simply apply his theory or seek to critically develop it (see Dowling in press for a discussion of this). This is complicated by Bernstein's tendency to strongly criticize those who, in his opinion, misappropriated his work (for example, see the introduction to Bernstein 1990 and Chapter 10 of Bernstein 2000). In this chapter, because I am interested in exploring what is offered by a Bernsteinian analysis of the relations between disciplinary knowledge practices and teaching–learning interactions, I mainly focus on applying Bernstein's approach. However, I also attempt to maintain a critical distance that allows me to examine the aspects of his approach that are less helpful in analysing the relations between disciplinary knowledge practices and teaching–learning interactions.

Conceptualizing disciplinary knowledge practices from a Bernsteinian perspective

Bernstein's concept of the pedagogic device both gives a sense of the processes through which disciplinary knowledge practices are situated in the teaching–learning interaction and offers a way to characterize the teaching–learning interaction from the perspective of disciplinary knowledge practices. Maton and Muller (2007, p. 19) summarize the Pedagogic Device as follows:

> . . . the ordered regulation and distribution of a society's worthwhile store of knowledge, ordered by a specifiable set of *distribution rules*; the transformation of this store into a pedagogic discourse, a form amenable to pedagogic transmission, ordered by a specifiable set of *recontextualizing rules*; and the further transformation of this peda-gogic discourse into a set of evaluative criteria to be attained, ordered by a specifiable set of *evaluative rules*. (emphasis in the original)

Thus, as Singh (2002) argues, the pedagogic device brings together an analysis of the macro and micro structuring of knowledge by relating the contexts in which knowledge is produced (distribution rules), made ready for transmission through the recontextualizing of that knowledge into a pedagogic discourse (recontextualizing rules), and is reproduced through pedagogic practice (evaluation rules). These rules are organized hierarchically, so that the distribution rules limit what is possible in relation to the recontextualizing rules, which in term provide limits for the evaluation rules (Bernstein 1999, 2000).

In line with the focus of previous chapters, I argue that together the distribution and recontextualizing rules provide an account of how disciplinary knowledge practices are situated in teaching–learning interactions, while the evaluation rules offer a way of analysing teaching–learning interactions from the perspective of disciplinary knowledge practices.

While the pedagogic device has mainly been examined from the perspective of the production and reproduction of school knowledge (for example, see Singh 2002), it is particularly interesting when one considers higher education (for an example, see Shay's 2008 analysis of assessment in higher education from the perspective of the pedagogic device). This is because in higher education, unlike school education, it is quite possible for the academics in higher education to be involved in the production, recontextualization and evaluation of the disciplinary knowledge practices and pedagogic discourses involved in the pedagogic device. However, as I will argue, the likelihood of this possibility being realized will vary between disciplinary knowledge practices and institutional settings. Wherever the rules of the pedagogic device are situated, it is important to recognize that the pedagogic device is an area of struggle over how academics' and students' ways of thinking will be structured through pedagogic discourse and whose interests will be served through this structuring (Bernstein 1990, 2000; Singh 2002; Maton and Muller 2007).

I first examine how the distribution and recontextualization rules provide a way of analysing how disciplinary knowledge practices are situated in teaching–learning interactions, before examining how the evaluation rules provide a way of conceptualizing teaching–learning interactions from the perspective of disciplinary knowledge practices.

Situating disciplinary knowledge practices in teaching–learning interactions

In examining how the distribution rules and recontextualizing rules situate disciplinary knowledge practices in teaching–learning interactions, I foreground the disciplinary aspects of these rules. As I have already discussed, each set of rules is a site of conflict and it is important to be clear that while I focus mainly on the disciplinary aspects of this conflict, it is also possible to highlight the institutional and political aspects of the conflicts over the control of these rules.

Distribution rules

The distribution rules of the pedagogic device govern 'who may transmit what to whom, and under what conditions' (Bernstein 1990, p. 183). In terms of analysing how disciplinary knowledge practices are situated in teaching–learning interactions in higher education, the distribution rules represent a site of struggle over *what* can legitimately be taught in universities, *who* may legitimately take on the role of a 'teacher' or 'learner', and the conditions under which teaching–learning processes take place.

The struggle over the '*what*' of higher education can be seen to take place in two different kinds of processes. First, there is a struggle within and between groupings of disciplinary knowledge practices over what count as legitimate knowledge practices. Thus it is possible to examine the ways in which new disciplinary knowledge practices develop their legitimacy in relation to existing disciplinary knowledge practices, for example Cultural Studies (Maton 2000a,b); Women's Studies (Coate 2006); and Computer Science (Clark 2006). Second, there are debates over which disciplinary knowledge practices should be the focus of higher education programmes, which as well as those within the field of higher education, involve those from other fields such as politics and employment. For example, in 2003 in the UK, the then Minister for Higher Education, Margaret Hodge, started a media debate about 'Mickey Mouse' degrees, degrees which she said lacked rigour and application to the employment market and so were not appropriate for higher education (for a discussion of Hodge's approach, see Sinfield *et al.* 2004, and for the development of the debate see Tahir 2007).

In relation to '*who* can teach *whom*', from the perspective of disciplinary knowledge practices, Maton (2000a,b, 2004, 2006, 2007a) has developed Bernstein's theory to argue that disciplinary discourses have a 'knower' structure that reflects who can have access to particular discourses. Maton (2004) argues that, compared to the natural sciences where anyone can come to know if they gain knowledge of specialist techniques, the social sciences have hierarchical knower structures because special attributes are required of those who wish to become legitimate knowers. Thus Maton argues that disciplinary knowledge practices may contain assumptions about who is a legitimate knower, which would impact on what qualities and qualifications are required to legitimately teach and learn a discipline, assumptions that Maton (2007a) argues are recognized by students themselves. However, such disciplinary views of 'who can teach whom' may be in conflict with, among others, those of higher education institutions, professional bodies, political and economic institutions over what is the appropriate focus of, and who should benefit from, higher education (for a UK-based example see Jones and Thomas's 2005 analysis of the 2003 Higher Education White Paper).

In terms of the *conditions* under which programmes are taught, Nespor (1994, 2007) examines the different ways in which time and space are constituted in different discipline knowledge practices. However, through debates and policy relating to what counts as higher education, government and other agencies can have a huge impact over the conditions defined by the distribution rules. For example, with the introduction of Foundation Degrees in England, there has been an increase in the delivery of higher education in further education institutions, as well as increased employer involvement in the design and delivery of higher education programmes, which have had an impact on the conditions under which higher education programmes are taught (see Wilson *et al.* 2005; Parry 2006; Reeve *et al.* 2007; Bathmaker *et al.* 2008; Thurgate and MacGregor 2008; for similar debates in Australia see Zipin 1999).

In this way, the distribution rules can be seen to play a role in situating disciplinary knowledge practices in teaching–learning interactions because they govern what counts as legitimate knowledge practices that can be taught and learned in higher education, who count as legitimate knowers, and what the conditions are under which this knowledge should be taught and learned. Thus differences in distribution rules can mean that in different institutions, the same disciplinary knowledge practices can be taught and studied under very different conditions and by students and academics with very different identities.

Recontextualizing rules

For Bernstein (1990, 2000) recontextualizing rules govern the transformation of legitimate knowledge into pedagogic discourse, that is to say the transformation of disciplinary knowledge practices into 'teachable' material. For Bernstein (1990, pp. 183–4), pedagogic discourse:

> removes (delocates) a discourse from its substantive practice and context, and relocates that discourse according to its own principle of selective reordering and focusing. In this process of the delocation and relocation of the original discourse, the social basis of its practice, including its power relations, is removed. In the process of the de- and relocation the original discourse is subject to a transformation which transforms it from an actual practice to a virtual practice. Pedagogic discourse creates imaginary subjects.

There are two elements to the recontextualization of disciplinary knowledge practices. These are their 'classification', the extent to which disciplinary knowledge practices maintain their specialized voices, and their 'framing', the processes by which these recontextualized voices are transformed into the messages of the curriculum.

In terms of the classification element of the recontextualization of disciplinary knowledge practices, Bernstein (2000) examines three broad ways in which they can be recontextualized into pedagogic discourse. First, they can be recontextualized as singulars, in which disciplines maintain their unique voice through strong classification, as they are 'insulated' from the discourses of other disciplines. Second, where classification is weak, Bernstein (2000, p. 9) argues that discourses are likely to be recontextualized as regions, which involve the recontextualization of different singulars in relation to each other. Whereas singulars are pure disciplines that are only focused on defining the problems generated by their own discourses, regions are more focused on dealing with problems generated in the world outside of the discipline (Beck 2002). Finally, where the voice of the discipline is very weak, there are generic modes that are focused on developing 'trainability' in students (Bernstein 2000, 2001; Beck and Young 2005). Bernstein (2000) argues that such modes are empty because they simply refer to themselves and are focused on responding to the changing demands of technology, organizations and the market. These modes can be seen in the promotion of 'generic skills' or 'learning-to-learn' programmes. Moore (2000) explores the introduction of generic competencies across a foundation course in the humanities in a South African university and illustrates the risks posed by their emptiness.

Bernstein (2000) suggests that an institution's position in the field of higher education will affect the processes of classification through which disciplinary knowledge discourses are recontextualized into pedagogic discourse. He argues that while 'elite' universities will retain a focus on singulars because their reputations will allow them to compete by attracting internationally renowned researchers, non-elite universities will compete by focusing on regions and putting different units of discourse together to create new packages of knowledge that are attractive to prospective students and employers (cf. Bourdieu's analysis of the higher education field in Chapter 7). This is supported by Abbas and McLean (2007a,b) who argue that the disciplinary knowledge of sociology is positioned differently in different institutions, with it being maintained as a singular in 'elite' institutions, while it increasingly becomes a region in other institutions as programmes shift from pure sociology to more applied programmes such as criminology. Related to this, Moore (2003) and Ensor (2004) explore the differences in the way different types of institution responded to a national policy in South Africa that sought to weaken the insulation between disciplines in order to open up access to higher education. However, it is important to recognize that it is not solely institutional differences that determine the classification of disciplinary knowledge practices within the curriculum. First, as Bernstein (2000, p. 55) recognizes, and Beck and Young (2005) discuss in detail, there are the 'classical university regions' such as medicine and engineering, which have always been taught in 'elite' universities. Second, as Clegg and Bradley (2006) argue in their examination of the implementation of Personal Development Planning in a single UK university, within institutions there can be different ways of dealing with the tension between the focus on disciplinary knowledge practices for their own sake and a focus on the relevance of such knowledge for the graduate employment market.

The framing element of recontextualization focuses on the processes through which disciplinary knowledge practices are transformed into higher education curriculum. For Bernstein (1990, 2000) decisions over the framing of curriculum, that is the selection, sequencing, pacing, criteria of, and the relations between academics and students within, the curriculum, are not simply based on the logic of the disciplinary discourse. Rather, this is again an area of struggle over the way in which the discipline is recontextualized. It is for this reason that Bernstein (1990, 2000) and Maton and Muller (2007) argue that knowledge structures are not the same curriculum structures. However, the precise relation between knowledge and curriculum structure is unclear. As Muller (2006, 2007) argues, there is clearly some relation, because, for example, there is some relation between students' performance in Mathematics across school and higher education and outside of educational contexts (i.e. their performance in relation to the disciplinary and pedagogic discourses). It seems likely that how close this relation remains is dependent on the dominant voices in determining the rules for recontextualizing disciplinary knowledge into curriculum. What is clear is that Bernstein's (1990, 2000) recontextualizing rules turn the relation between higher education curriculum and disciplinary knowledge into a site for struggle.

Thus the relations are contingent and changeable and their form becomes an empirical question rather than it being assumed that there is a clear and consistent relation between the two.

The processes through which the framing of disciplinary knowledge discourses into curriculum takes place are again the sites of struggle between academics, institutions, disciplinary and professional bodies and the employment field, as well as government agencies. For example, in the UK subject benchmark statements published by the Quality Assurance Agency set out the nature and defining principles of disciplinary knowledge practices, appropriate approaches to teaching–learning processes in particular disciplines and standards that students should be expected to reach (see Hodson and Thomas 2003 for an account of their development). However, such quality frameworks may work differently in different institutions (for example, see Abbas and McLean 2007b; Brennan and Osborne 2008). Another factor that might vary between disciplinary knowledge practices is the extent to which recontextualization takes place within individual institutions, on a national level or on an international level for particular levels of programmes. For example, at undergraduate level the recontextualization of some forms of disciplinary knowledge practices takes place in the form of national or international textbooks, which academics base their lectures around (for example, see Nespor's 1994 account of Physics, and Dowling 1998 for an in-depth analysis of the recontextualization of mathematics in school textbooks). In relation to other disciplinary practices, such as those involved in medicine and engineering, national professional and regulatory bodies may play an important role in determining what is included in the curriculum (for example, see O'Connor's 2008 analysis of the pedagogic discourse of nursing). Finally, there may be less regulated disciplines in which academics decide what to include in their curricula based on their conceptions and interests in the discipline. These different ways in which disciplinary knowledge practices are recontextualized into pedagogic discourses may have an impact on the relation between an academic's research interest and the material they are teaching in that the more local the recontextualization, the more space they have to draw on their disciplinary specialisms.

The distribution and recontextualizing rules of the pedagogic device offer the tools to analyse the way in which disciplinary knowledge practices are situated in teaching–learning interactions. While a

Community of Practice perspective appears to assume that there is an unproblematic relationship between discipline-as-research and discipline-as-curriculum, the distribution and recontextualizing rules show how both disciplinary knowledge practices become part of higher education programmes and the processes through which these disciplinary knowledge practices are transformed into curriculum are the sites of struggle and contestation. My analysis of the distribution and recontextualizing rules suggests that the way in which disciplinary knowledge practices are situated in teaching–learning interactions will vary not only according to the characteristics of the disciplinary knowledge practices, but also in relation to their institutional settings.

Characterizing teaching–learning interactions in terms of disciplinary knowledge practices

In thinking about how teaching–learning interactions can be conceptualized in terms of disciplinary knowledge practices, I turn to the evaluation rules, the third set of rules of the pedagogic device. The evaluation rules are focused on the transformation of pedagogic discourse into pedagogic practice. From Bernstein's (2000) perspective, the key to pedagogic practice is the continuous evaluation, or assessment, of whether students are creating the legitimate 'texts' demanded by the pedagogic discourse. By 'text' Bernstein is referring to forms of evidence that the aspect of curriculum has been acquired, which may not necessarily be a physical text. It is evaluation rules that govern the production of these texts (Bernstein 1990) and they regulate pedagogic practice because they define the standards that the students must reach in their studies. In this way, the evaluation rules are set more locally than the distribution or recontextualizing rules, and are generally focused on how academics and students interpret the curriculum that is produced through the recontextualizing rules.

It is important to be clear that Bernstein (1990, 2000) argues that the three sets of rules exist in a hierarchical relationship, so that the recontextualizing rules are derived from the distribution rules, and the evaluation rules are derived from the recontextualizing rules. This means that using the evaluation rules to characterize the teaching–learning interaction rests upon the understanding of the processes through which disciplinary knowledge processes are situated in teaching–learning interactions outlined in the previous section. Thus in examining how teaching–learning interactions can be characterized in terms of disciplinary knowledge practices, I am examining how teaching–learning interactions can be characterized in terms of pedagogic discourse. There are two aspects to this. First, there are the models of pedagogic practice that are developed from pedagogic discourse, which position students and academics in particular ways. Second, there are the ways in which students and academics respond to these discourses, which Bernstein (1990, 2000) argues is based on their 'knowledge codes'. In examining these two aspects, I argue that they provide a way of characterizing the teaching–learning interaction in terms of disciplinary knowledge practices that, unlike a Communities of Practice perspective, does not assume that students and academics are part of the same disciplinary community, and offers a way of analysing power within these interactions.

The recontextualization of disciplinary knowledge practices into pedagogic discourse will shape the models of pedagogic practice that inform teaching–learning interactions. Bernstein (1975, 1990, 2000) develops two models of pedagogic practice: performance or visible pedagogies and competence or invisible pedagogies.

Bernstein (1990) argues that visible pedagogies are performance models of curricula. They are based on strong classification and framing. Thus, in relation to higher education, within performance models there is a strong separation between disciplinary knowledge practices, between educational knowledge and everyday knowledge, and between academics and students with teaching–learning interactions. Thus Bernstein (2000) argues that within such performance models the focus is on something that the student acquirer does not possess and an emphasis on the text that students need to acquire and therefore academics need to transmit. The emphasis of assessment in performance pedagogies is on the performance of each student, the text they need to produce, and on establishing the differences between students. Thus the text to be produced is explicit and there is a strict timeframe in which it needs to be produced (Bernstein 1990). The academics' teaching professionalism lies in their ability to be explicit in their approach to teaching the required text and their skill in grading the texts that students produce in comparison to the required text.

Bernstein (1990) characterizes invisible pedagogies as competence models of curricula. Thus, while in performance models the focus is on the relative performance of each student, within competence models the focus is on the competence of each individual student. Thus students appear to fill the pedagogic space because the focus is on assessing the extent to which internal procedures are taking place within each student. Thus the academic's role and expertise are related to decoding the texts that students produce in order to establish what has occurred within that student. While classification and framing *appear* to be weak within competence models, there is still a range of texts that are appropriate for students to produce because, despite its apparent openness, the situation is still an educational one. The extent to which students recognize this will depend on their understanding of the teaching–learning interaction, an issue I will discuss in more detail below.

Bernstein (2000) suggests that all pedagogies in higher education are likely to be performance pedagogies with students required to produce clearly defined texts within a specified timeframe. However, this may well depend on the particular knowledge practices. In general, it seems likely that particular examples of pedagogic practice in higher education may be made up of different combinations of performance and competence models. The particular model of pedagogic practice that is developed will depend on both the disciplinary knowledge practices and how they have been recontextualized into curriculum.

In terms of the disciplinary knowledge practices, it seems plausible that the more the knower code dominates the knowledge code (Maton 2004), the more likely that pedagogic modes will be focused on interpreting what has occurred within the student rather than assessing highly defined and visible texts. Examples of disciplinary knowledge practices where the text produced is intended to represent the internal processes of the practitioner may include *some* aspects of the knowledge practices in Art and Design (for example, see contributions to Drew 2008) and Music (Dibben 2006).

Clearly the recontextualization of disciplinary knowledge practices will depend on the practices that are recontextualized. In general, where they are recontextualized into singulars, there is more likely to be a greater emphasis on students demonstrating their mastery of the disciplinary knowledge practices through a performance-based pedagogy. However, where pedagogic discourse regionalizes knowledge, it appears there is likely to be more space for competence-based pedagogies, in terms of focusing on the characteristics developed by the students in order to relate the different recontextualized disciplinary discourses. Within generic discourses, because they are empty in terms of their disciplinary knowledge practices, they will focus entirely on the 'train-ability' of the students rather than their production of disciplinary texts (Bernstein 2001).

Thus it appears likely that as curricula shift from singulars to regions to generic modes, there is an accompanying shift from mainly per-formance or visible pedagogies towards a greater degree of compe-tence or invisible pedagogies. Thus there is a shift from a focus on a text that students need to be able to produce to a focus on the internal processes within each student, which the academic must decode in order to establish what has been achieved.

While the relations between pedagogic discourse and modes of peda-gogic practice can be seen to create ideal pedagogic identities for academics and students, how these play out through teaching–learning interactions will be related to students' and academics' orientations to knowledge or knowledge codes. Bernstein (1990) argues that a person's knowledge code generates principles for distinguishing between contexts (recognition rules), a matter of classification, and principles for the creation and production of the legitimate messages within contexts (realization rules), a matter of framing. Thus the meaning that students and academics give to particular teaching–learning inter-actions is generated through the relations between their orientation to knowledge (their code) and the way in which disciplinary knowledge practices have been recontextualized in terms of pedagogic discourses and models of pedagogic practice. In relation to school education, Bern-stein (1999) argues that there are class-based differences in students' orientations to knowledge that impact on their understanding of educational interactions. The extent to, and ways in which, these play a role in students' experiences of teaching–learning interactions in higher education is an interesting question.

Students' and academics' responses to recontextualized disciplinary knowledge practices are related to what they understand the interaction to be about and how they produce their own texts within these inter-actions. Abbas and McLean's (2007b, p. 17) analysis of pedagogic iden-tities among sociology lecturers suggests that while there is pressure on academics in less privileged institutions towards more regionalized pedagogic discourses, their commitment to their disciplinary knowledge practices meant that 'for *all* the lecturers good pedagogic quality is the space and capacity to make adjustments to preserve and to communicate to students core academic and disciplinary values'.

Within a Bernsteinian characterization of teaching–learning interactions in terms of disciplinary knowledge practices, there is a focus on the relations between the types of texts that students are required to produce, the role of the academic in assisting in the development and assessment of these texts, and the students' and academics' orientations to knowledge. Thus teaching–learning interactions are seen as the playing out of these relations, and will follow different paths according to the ways in which these factors impact on each other. Such a view of teaching–learning interactions does not involve an assumption that students and academics are part of the same disciplinary community; rather, it focuses on their different relations to recontextualized disciplinary knowledge practices. In doing so, it emphasizes the differences in their positions in teaching–learning interactions and highlights issues of how power and control are exercised through classification and framing respectively.

The possibilities of a Bernsteinian analysis of the relations between disciplinary knowledge practices and teaching–learning interactions

I have argued that Bernstein's approach highlights the processes through which disciplinary knowledge practices are produced and transformed into curriculum, as well as the processes through which different disciplines and higher education institutions might offer very different 'higher educations'. Finally, rather than assuming that students and academics are part of the same disciplinary community, it highlights the processes through which academics and students are differently positioned in teaching–learning interactions.

This has three implications for those interested in researching different aspects of the relationship between disciplinary setting and teaching–learning interactions. First, in problematizing the relationship between disciplinary knowledge practices and pedagogic discourses, it raises some interesting questions about approaches that seek to examine how students engage with disciplinary knowledge practices. For example, much of the focus on 'threshold concepts' (see Chapter 3, and Meyer and Land 2005) in higher education examines students' issues with particular concepts as if this knowledge comes directly from knowledge discourses. However, highlighting how this knowledge is transformed into pedagogic discourse raises a series of different questions about the reasons for students' difficulty. Thus rather than focusing on inherent difficulties within particular disciplinary knowledge practices, a Bernsteinian approach raises questions about how this knowledge has been recontextualized into the curriculum. Is it how this knowledge has been positioned, sequenced and paced in relation to the rest of the curriculum that causes students difficulty? Is it the processes through which the practices of the discipline have been transformed into virtual practices that causes students difficulty in developing their understanding of disciplinary knowledge? For example, Maton (2007b) argues, in his analysis of 'authentic learning environments', that students can sometimes be left with knowledge that is rooted in the context of particular cases and cannot be applied to other contexts because they have not developed the principles on which to recontextualize their knowledge.

Second, a Bernsteinian approach questions the assumptions of large-scale studies that examine disciplinary differences in teaching–learning processes (for example, Neumann 2001; Neumann *et al.* 2002; Brint *et al.* 2008; Nelson Laird *et al.* 2008). This is because these studies rely on the assumption that Becher (1989) and Becher and Trowler's (2001) typology, which was developed in relation to disciplines-as-research, is applicable to disciplines-as-curriculum. As I have argued in this chapter, a Bernsteinian approach suggests that the same disciplinary knowledge practices may take on very different characteristics when it is recontextualized into curriculum and that different disciplines may be subject to different forms of recontextualization. This suggests that the relationship between discipline-as-research and discipline-as-curriculum is more complex and contingent than is suggested by statistical correlations between students' experiences of teaching–learning processes and the discipline they are studying. While Trowler (2008b) recognizes this in his critique of 'epistemological essentialism' (the notion that disciplinary knowledge practices determine teaching–learning practices), the pedagogic device gives a more developed sense of the structuring processes involved in the transformation of disciplinary knowledge into curriculum than Trowler's (2008b) injunction to consider the dynamics of the particular departmental context, including its local history and culture. Thus while Trowler (2008b) emphasizes the local factors that shape the way in which curricula are produced, a Bernsteinian approach emphasizes how this process can involve the interweaving of local, national and global processes which together give apparently the same disciplinary knowledge practices different structures in different institutions.

Finally, the pedagogic device highlights that the ways in which different disciplinary knowledge practices are recontextualized can be very different depending on the institutional location of each set of rules. Thus for some disciplinary knowledge practices, in some institutions, the recontextualization can largely be decided outside of the institution through the use of particular textbooks or the requirements of accrediting professional bodies. For others, the recontexualization of disciplinary knowledge practices into curriculum is likely to be a more local affair, thus giving academics more space in which to relate the curriculum to their research specialisms and to the interests and learning needs of their students. It seems possible that the level of control and ownership that academics have of the recontextualization of disciplinary knowledge practices into curriculum is highly significant in shaping academics' and students' experiences of teaching–learning interactions in higher education.

The tensions in a Bernsteinian analysis of the relations between disciplinary knowledge practices and teaching–learning interactions

The main tension in a Bernsteinian approach to analysing the relations between disciplinary knowledge practices and teaching–learning interactions is related to the way in which the teaching–learning interaction is characterized in terms of disciplinary knowledge practices. In characterizing the teaching–learning interaction as the relations between the mode of pedagogic practice and the knowledge codes of students and academics, it is difficult to gain a sense of how these relations might shift in dynamic ways over the course of a particular interaction. This means that it is not clear how students and academics might respond to particular sets of relations and how these might change over time. Bernstein

(1990, p. 6) recognized that this was related to his focus on the system but argued 'the system does not create copper-etched plates'. As Diaz (2001, pp. 94–5) argues, the Bernstein approach de-centres the subject because:

> the basic empirical and conceptual unit of his work is not an individual subject but a relationship, a pedagogic relationship through which a subject emerges. Thus the subject is contingent on the pedagogic relation, while the consequence of the pedagogic relation is contingent on the response of the subject to that relation.

This suggests that the response to this tension would be to examine empirical examples of how these relations emerge and shift over the course of particular teaching–learning interactions so that particular illustrations of these contingent outcomes can be developed. What should be noted is that within this characterization there is a clear sense of the different practices of academics and students within these interactions, but this is achieved while maintaining a focus on the interaction as a shared activity. Thus while it does not provide an immediate sense of the dynamic and shifting aspects of these interactions, it does allow a focus on the intimately related, but differently focused, activities of students and academics within teaching–learning interactions.

Conclusion

In this chapter, I have explored how adopting a Bernsteinian perspective to analysing the relations between disciplinary knowledge practices and teaching–learning interactions addresses the limitations of a Communities of Practice approach to analysing these relations. I have suggested that in problematizing the relation between discipline-as-research and discipline-as-curriculum this analysis highlights the processes in which curricula are produced and the different ways in which the same disciplinary knowledge practices may be recontextualized. Finally, I argued that while a Bernsteinian analysis does not currently provide a sense of the dynamic and shifting aspects of teaching–learning interactions, this might be developed through an examination of particular empirical examples of the relations between pedagogic discourse, modes of pedagogic practice and the knowledge codes of students and academics.

Chapter 7

Analysing the relations between institutional cultures and teaching–learning interactions

Introduction

In this chapter I consider how to analyse the relations between institutional cultures and teaching–learning interactions. I examine how these relations can be analysed by drawing on Pierre Bourdieu's notions of 'field', 'capital' and '*habitus*'. I first examine my reasons for adopting a Bourdieusian perspective, before introducing some of his key ideas. I then focus on how Bourdieu's approach enables an analysis of how institutional cultures are situated in teaching–learning interactions and how it can be used to conceptualize teaching–learning interactions in terms of institutional cultures. Finally, I explore the possibilities and tensions within a Bourdieusian analysis of the relations between institutional cultures and teaching–learning interactions.

Why examine a Bourdieusian approach to analysing the relations between institutional cultures and teaching–learning interactions?

In Chapter 3, I examined Teaching and Learning Regimes (Trowler 2005, 2008) as a way of analysing the relations between institutional cultures and teaching–learning interactions, and argued that there were two problems with this approach. First, while it gives a sense of how institutional cultures are shaped by the particular locale, it does not give a sense of the institutional cultures themselves. This means that it does not offer a sense of the differences between institutional cultures or an explanation of their origins. Second, it does not provide a sense of how teaching–learning interactions can be characterized in terms of institutional cultures.

There are four reasons for examining the work of Bourdieu when attempting to account for the relations between institutional cultures and teaching–learning interactions in higher education. First, through his concepts of 'field', 'capital' and '*habitus*', he offers a way of analysing how the position of higher education institutions within the field of higher education impact on their institutional cultures or, in Bourdieusian terms, their organizational or institutional *habitus* (see McDonough 1997; Reay 1998). This provides at least a partial account of some of the origins of the differences between institutional cultures. Second, the notions of 'higher education field' and 'institutional *habitus*' provide a way of analysing how institutional cultures are situated in teaching–learning interactions and how teaching–learning interactions can be conceptualized from the perspective of institutional cultures. Third, Bourdieu's and his colleagues' research involved an examination of aspects of teaching–learning processes. Bourdieu conducted several empirical studies into French higher education (Bourdieu 1988; 1996; Bourdieu and Passeron, 1979; 1990; Bourdieu *et al.* 1994) and this work is being used to inform research into a number of aspects of higher and further education including teaching–learning interactions (for example, see James 2000; Hodkinson and James 2003; Reay *et al.* 2005; Shay 2005; Lucas 2006; James *et al.* 2007; Crozier *et al.* 2008). Finally, Bourdieu's work is explicitly concerned with addressing the, for Bourdieu, false divide between approaches focused on social structure and approaches focused on individual agency:

> Of all the oppositions that artificially divide social science, the most fundamental, and the most ruinous, is the one that is set up between subjectivism and objectivism. The very act that this division constantly reappears in virtually the same form would suffice to indicate that the modes of knowledge which it distinguishes are equally indispensable to a science of the social world. (Bourdieu 1990a, p. 25)

Bourdieu's concepts of 'field', 'capital' and '*habitus*'

The concepts of 'field', 'capital' and '*habitus*' are central to Bourdieu's analysis of the social world. A field is a network of objective relations between *positions* occupied by agents or institutions (see Bourdieu and Waquant 1992). In his empirical work, Bourdieu examined a wide range of fields including the field of science (Bourdieu 2004), the field of cultural production (Bourdieu 1993), the field of the French housing market (Bourdieu 2005) and the field of Parisian higher education (Bourdieu 1988). Each field is semi-autonomous from the overall field of power, a meta-field which, in part, encompasses all of the other fields (Bourdieu and Wacquant 1992). This means that as they enter into particular fields, processes, such as government policy, are refracted and retranslated into the terms that are at stake in that field.

The positions of agents or institutions within a particular field are defined by the distribution of specific forms of *capital* that are at stake in the *game* of that field. The game in the field involves agents in 'trying' to maintain or develop particular forms of capital that are valued in that field or to change the implicit rules of the field so that the capital they are strong in is valued. It is important to note that what are important in the game are not the relations between agents but the objective relations between *positions*, in terms of the amount and forms of capital that they hold (Bourdieu and Waquant 1992).

The forms of capital at stake vary between and within fields. There are three main forms of capital: economic, cultural and social, but these take on different forms of symbolic capital, the form they take on when they are recognized within the game of particular field (Bourdieu and Waquant 1992; see Moore 2004 for a discussion). If Bourdieu's use of these terms can seem to change between texts, then it is because he sees the definition of what forms of capital are at stake in a particular field as an empirical matter rather than something to be defined theoretically (Bourdieu and Waquant 1992).

However, the games are not experienced by social agents in terms of the maintenance and accumulation of particular forms of capital. Rather, they have a 'feel for the game' that is unconscious and is engendered by their *habitus*. The *habitus* is a system of durable dispositions that are developed in social agents through their past experiences (a 'structured structure') but that is also used to make sense of new experiences (a 'structuring structure') (Bourdieu 1990a).

The *habitus* is a 'structured structure' in that it is developed through agents' passed experiences, with childhood experiences particularly important. Bourdieu is not simply referring to cognitive structures here; rather the categories, concepts and bodily postures that social agents develop over time serve to make some things appear possible and other things unthinkable. Social agents are not necessarily conscious of their *habitus* or the ways in which it is structured; Bourdieu (1990a, p. 56) refers to the *habitus* 'as a forgetting of history'. Finally, because the categories that individuals used are not their own, because they do not invent them, and because early material conditions play an important role in structuring the *habitus*, each individual's *habitus* is a structural variant of that of other members of their social class. Thus for Bourdieu the *habitus* represents the internalization of the external structures relating to social class.

The *habitus* is also a 'structuring structure' because the dispositions that it develops define the limits of what social agents consider think-able and doable in their lives. According to Bourdieu, the operation of the *habitus* results in the selective perception of social agents, and it operates in such a way that individuals tend to confirm and reinforce their past experiences rather than challenge them. In this way social agents develop an implicit sense of the probabilities of various events occurring in their lives (for example, going to university or getting a particular type of job) and 'cut their coat to suit their cloth'. In fact, they can revel in their limited opportunities as the sorts of things that 'people like us' do or don't do. Finally the *habitus* is the device through which agents carry their cultural capital into particular fields.

There are a number of issues about field, capital and *habitus* that need to be emphasized. First, it should be clear that for Bourdieu field, *habitus* and capital only operate in relation to each other (Bourdieu and Waquant 1992). Thus a field necessarily involves social agents in trying to maintain or develop different forms of capital; these forms of capital only have value in relation to a field, and the *habitus* of social agents only operate in relation to specific fields. It is in this way that Bourdieu sees his analysis as *relational*, that is, focused on the objective relations between the positions of social agents in the field, in which the objective relations are defined by the distribution of capital at stake in that field (Bourdieu and Waquant 1992).

Second, field, *habitus* and capital are not concepts that are to be mapped theoretically. Rather, the relations between them are to be explored empirically through the collection and analysis of data. Thus in discussing the limits of a particular field, Bourdieu is clear that this is an empirical matter rather than a question of an assumption on the part of the researcher. This is partly because the limits of the field are always at stake within the game, because these limits can help to define the value of the capital held by social agents (Bourdieu and Waquant 1992).

Third, because for Bourdieu the purpose of social science is to explain how regularities are reproduced with the unknown 'complicity' of agents through their social practices, the role of social science research is to offer analyses of fields, to map out the objective structures of relations between the positions of agents and to analyse how the *habitus* of agents contributes to the reproduction or transformation of these fields (Bourdieu and Waquant 1992).

In this way, Bourdieu brings together the ideas of field, capital and *habitus* to offer a double reading of social agents' practices. Fields select and shape those who enter them so that their *habitus* fit with the logic of the games that they involve, while social agents' position in the field (i.e. their distribution of capital) influences the view they take on the field and the strategies they adopt in order to maintain and develop their capital. When there is a perfect fit between *habitus* and the field, *doxa* is established. *Doxa* is 'the relation of immediate adherence that is established in practice between a *habitus* and the field in which it is attuned, the pre-verbal taking for granted of the world that flows from practical sense' (Bourdieu 1990a, p. 68).

Thus Bourdieu brings together objectivist accounts and subjectivist accounts to offer an explanation of the regularity of social agents' practices in terms of the fit between *habitus* and field. Again, it is important to emphasize that this fit is not a conscious one on the part of social agents and that they are not aware of the regularity in their practices or the way in which this is achieved. Social practices are not reproduced by strategic calculations but rather by the unreflective everyday non-decisions that agents 'make' every day. Thus, 'it is because subjects do not, strictly speaking, know what they are doing that what they do has more meaning than they know' (Bourdieu 1977, p. 79). Thus in Bourdieu's terms, agents often *misrecognize* the objective purposes of their actions.

It is important to recognize that this is not a determinist account of the regularities found in social practices. First, change can happen. Indeed, *Homo Academicus* (Bourdieu 1988) is partly an account of how increases in the number of university teachers and students led to the student revolts in 1968, precisely because of lack of fit between the *habitus* of the new types of academics and students and what the field of higher education could offer. Second, Bourdieu is clear that it is not inevitable that the regularities in the field will be reproduced. They are reproduced by the actions of agents and there is always the possibility that social agents might act differently – it is just unlikely when *habitus* and fields are aligned. Thus Bourdieu is careful to use phrases such as 'everything takes place as if' and 'resembles' when describing the regularities in fields.

Conceptualizing institutional cultures from a Bourdieusian perspective

In this section I examine how Bourdieu's notions of field, capital and *habitus* might be applied to understand how the institutional culture impacts on teaching–learning interactions in higher education. Using these notions it is possible to consider the positions of different higher education institutions in the field of higher education and how these positions impact on their institutional *habitus*.

The field of higher education

The field of higher education can be conceived as a game in which different players compete in order to maintain and develop different types of capital. In thinking about institutions, the focus is on the position of different institutions with this field. For example, Marginson (2008) explores the global field of higher education and, drawing on Bourdieu (1993), divides the field of higher education institutions along two axes. The first axis is a continuum from elite research universities to commercial vocational education, and the second axis is a focus on global or local markets (see Marginson 2008, Figure 1, p. 306). The continuums of the axes are hierarchical. Elite research universities have more autonomy to generate their own problems while commercial vocational institutions have a number of different rulers (heteronomy) (see Grenfell and James 2004 for a discussion of autonomy and heteronomy in fields).

However, the notion of field is dynamic. Thus institutions try to position themselves and develop their forms of capital within this field. There are a number of elements to this. First, not all institutions are attempting to develop the same forms of capital. Zipin (1999) argues, in an analysis of the responses of different institutions to higher education reform in Australia, that 'elite' institutions attempt to focus debates on the importance of 'elite' education while other institutions argue that higher education needs to be vocationally relevant. Thus under Bordieu's analysis, the position of a higher education institution in the field of higher education will shape which forms of capital it seeks to maintain and develop. As Zipin (1999) argues, part of this game of developing capital is to attempt to define higher education in such a way that the sort of capital an institution is strong in is defined as 'the main game' of higher education. This means that while there is a hierarchy of institutions, it is not the case that those lower in the hierarchy accept the terms of the more dominant. Rather, as Robbins (1993) argues, all institutions attempt to define 'higher education' in a way that validates their approach, whether or not they are 'elite' institutions.

Second, as Hodkinson *et al.* (2007, 2008) argue in relation to English further education, the field of higher education is seen as having relative autonomy from other fields, such as employment and government policy. Maton (2005) argues that the development of the notion of the 'new student' in the UK in response to the 1963 Robbins report into higher education was a refracted form of other external pressures. Thus government policy and the views of employers can have an impact on what counts as higher education or even what counts as a higher education institution. For example, as I discussed in Chapter 6, in England the introduction of foundation degrees by the government has changed the sense of not only what counts as a degree but also where such degrees are taught and learned (similarly see James *et al.* 2007 for a consideration of the different players in the field of English further education). Thus the notion of the boundary of higher education is a key site for conflict within the field.

Third, as Naidoo (2004) argues in her analysis of the South African field of higher education and James *et al.* (2007) in their examination of further education, the same policy impacts differently on institutions depending on their position within the field of higher education. Similarly Marginson (2008) argues that 'elite' research universities have more autonomy than mass commercial vocational education institutions who are more subject to changes in policy or the views of employers. Again, to refer back to the example of foundation degrees, it is clear that 'elite' universities have ignored this form of higher education.

Institutional *habitus*

As I indicated earlier, the notion of organizational or institutional *habitus* has been developed in the work of McDonough (1997) and Reay (1998) (see also Reay *et al.* 2005 and, specifically in relation to higher education institutions, Thomas 2002 and Crozier *et al.* 2008). McDonough (1997) develops the concept as a link between institutions and the wider socioeconomic context, and it is this link that she argues differentiates institutional *habitus* from institutional culture. As I argued above, institutional *habitus* is developed in relation to each institution's position in the field of higher education. Thus the sorts of capital that different institutions are attempting to maintain or develop will inform institutional notions of what is 'reasonable'. As Bourdieu (2005, pp. 8–9) argues, the *habitus* involves:

> . . . dispositions acquired through learning processes associated with protracted dealings with the regularities of the field; apart from any conscious calculation, these dispositions are capable of generating behaviours and even anticipations which would be better termed *reasonable* than *rational.*

In her study of how US schools impact on their students' choice of college, McDonough (1997) argues that institutional *habitus* informs an institution's sense of who its students are expected to be, the sorts of courses that they will be offered and which progression routes constitute reasonable uses of the capital that students have developed. Reay *et al.* (2005) draw on McDonough's work in their study of higher education choice in the UK. They emphasize that students are positioned according to the level of congruence between their *habitus* and the institutional *habitus* of the school, they examine this congruence in terms of the educational status of the school, its organizational practices and its expressive order. In higher education, Thomas (2002) examines the impact that the congruence between individual and institutional *habitus* has on student retention.

In drawing on the notion of institutional *habitus*, there is one important difference in the way that I think about it. While McDonough (1997) and Reay *et al.* (2005) tend to present institutional *habitus* as directly related to a school's position in the field of education, my focus on teaching–learning interactions means that I am interested in how institutional *habitus* is refracted *within* higher educational institutions. Although the work of Bourdieu and his co-researchers in higher education tends to focus on the relations between the position of institutions and disciplines within the general field of higher education and the *habitus* and experiences of students and academics (for example, see Bourdieu 1988, 1996; Bourdieu and Passeron 1979, 1990; and Bourdieu *et al.* 1994), his work in other fields offers an alternative way of conceptualizing this relation. In his examination of the French housing market, Bourdieu (2005, p. 69) argues that as well as being 'guided' by their position in structure of the field of production, the 'choices' of agents are also 'guided' by their position in the internal field of their particular firm. In applying this approach to higher education, the impact that institutional *habitus* has on teaching–learning interactions will be mediated by where particular programmes of study are positioned within the field of the institution. The process through which this refraction occurs will depend on the particular structure of the institution. Thus in a university with an institutional structure which involves faculties and departments, institutional *habitus* will be shaped through the university's position in the field of higher education but it will then be refracted through the particular faculty's position in the institutional field, the department's position in the faculty field, and the programme of study's position in the departmental field. In institutions with different structures, the fields through which institutional *habitus* is refracted will be different.

There are three aspects of this approach that should be emphasized. First, the forms of symbolic capital that are valued in each of these sub-fields may be subtly different. Second, this means that the form of institutional *habitus* that is situated in teaching–learning interactions cannot simply be read off from the institution's position in the field of higher education and emphasizes the importance of careful empirical examination of the forms of symbolic capital that are at stake within these fields. Third, this approach to institutional *habitus* sits more comfortably with approaches to institutional cultures that emphasize that such cultures have multiple configurations and avoids the implication that institutions have single organizational cultures (for example, see Alvesson 2002).

Situating institutional cultures in teaching–learning interactions

So far I have argued that institutional cultures can be analysed in terms of institutional *habitus*. I have also argued that institutional *habitus* is refracted through a range of internal fields before it is situated in teaching–learning interactions. I now consider the forms through which institutional *habitus* is carried through these different fields. As these forms of the expression of institutional *habitus* move through these fields, their meanings for agents within each sub-field are likely to change depending on the forms of symbolic capital that are at stake in that particular field.

In considering the forms of expression of institutional *habitus* that situate it within teaching–learning interactions, I examine a number of ways in which these might be carried. As with the previous chapters, this examination is based on the outcomes of existing research into higher education. The factors I examine are not intended to be exhaustive or to always be significant in all institutions. Rather, my intention is to give a sense of the ways in which institutional *habitus* can be situated in teaching–learning interactions, but it is a matter for empirical investigation of how these work out in particular institutional settings.

I argue that institutional *habitus* can become situated in teaching–learning interactions through the selection criteria for entry to particular programmes, the particular form of the programmes that institutions offer, institutional teaching–learning quality regimes, institutional approaches to the development of teaching–learning processes, and the form of institutional teaching–learning spaces. I argue that each of these can be seen to situate institutional *habitus* within teaching–learning interactions.

Entry requirements for students and academics

One way in which institutional *habitus* can become situated within teaching–learning interactions is through informing who can legitimately become a student and an academic who teaches within particular programmes within particular institutions. In his work, Bourdieu emphasized the way in which disciplines within institutions select academics (Bourdieu 1988) and students (Bourdieu 1996) who will 'fit' (see also Naidoo 2004; Crozier *et al.* 2008). This is a two-sided process. In relation to students, research with 'non-traditional' students suggests that they can sometimes choose universities to which they feel they have the greatest chance of developing a sense of belonging (Read *et al.* 2003), which means seeing the institution as having a diversity of students in terms of maturity, ethnicity and social class. This two-sided process can be argued to be reflected in the lower levels of diversity among students in more privileged higher education institutions (Brennan and Osborne 2008).

The position of a university will also impact on the academics who are engaged in teaching. Bourdieu (1988) examined the relation between an institution's position in the field of Parisian higher education and the identities of academics within those institutions. The requirements for who can gain a post of a lecturer is different depending on a university's position in the field of higher education both in terms of formal qualifications and research and teaching experiences, and different academics may feel comfortable in different types of institutional settings (Henkel 2000).

In this way, institutional *habitus* is situated in teaching–learning interactions through informing which students and academics are involved in these interactions. As I argued above, these selection criteria are refracted through the different institutional fields in which the teaching–learning interaction is situated, such as the field of the programme itself, and the department and faculty who run the programme. This highlights, for example, how even within a single department the criteria for being a student and an academic who teaches on different programmes can be quite different.

Curriculum offer

As well as who is involved in teaching–learning interactions, institutional *habitus* becomes situated in teaching–learning interactions through the curriculum that is the focus of such interactions. As Mc-Donough (1998) argued in relation to schools, a university's position in the field of higher education can impact on the content of the programme. Abbas and McLean (2007a) argued that there were clear differences in the way that Sociology was presented in two institutions differently positioned in the field of higher education. Equally, the level of autonomy that academics have in structuring what and how they teach is likely to vary according to their university's position in the field of higher education (James 2007). Again, this will be refracted through a number of different fields within the institution, with the different forms of institutional capital that are at stake in the fields playing a role in informing the form of curriculum that is seen as 'reasonable' for the particular programme.

Quality regimes

The approach taken to assuring quality within teaching–learning interactions can be another way in which institutional *habitus* is situated in teaching–learning interactions. Although in the UK quality frameworks are set at a national level, with slightly different approaches in England, Scotland, Wales and Northern Ireland, in each case it is for institutions to implement these regimes. In England, Brennan and Osborne (2008) and Abbas and McLean (2007b) argued that there were differences in the way that such regimes were interpreted and implemented related to the type of institution involved. These approaches again seem to suggest a direct link between the institution's position in the field of higher education and their quality regimes, but I would stress the role that the fields *within* institutions play in leading particular institutional approaches to quality regimes being interpreted and implemented in different ways (see also Clegg and Bradley 2006 for differences in the implementation in Personal Development Planning within a single institution).

Teaching–learning development

Related to the quality regimes is the approach that is taken to developing teaching–learning processes within those institutions. For example, in England each higher education institution is expected to develop a Teaching and Learning Strategy that sets out their institutional approach to the development of learning and teaching (see Gibbs *et al.* 2000). These approaches will be informed by an institution's position in the field of higher education, and the forms of capital they are seeking to develop. There is some evidence for this in terms of the different approaches to educational development in different institutions (Gosling 2008). In relation to institutional teaching development programmes, Hanbury *et al.* (2008) argued that their data suggested that teaching development programmes were more positively received in newer higher education institutions and had a greater impact on teaching. This could be argued to reflect these institutions' focus on developing their capital in relation to teaching–learning processes more than capital related to research activity.

Similarly, there is evidence of institutional differences in approaches to supporting students' learning, with new universities more likely to offer generic, remedial student support which is separate from academic staff (Smith 2007; see also Crozier *et al.* 2008).

In this way, forms of institutional support for teaching–learning processes can be seen to reflect institutions' position within the field of higher education and to situate aspects of institutional *habitus* within teaching–learning interactions. Again, these will be refracted through fields internal to the institution. For example, the relation between departments and institutional teaching developments might reflect a particular department's position within the institutional field.

Time and space for teaching–learning processes

The final way in which institutional *habitus* can become situated in teaching–learning interactions that I consider is through the constitution of time and space in which these interactions take place. These can include assumptions about how students will spend their time preparing for sessions (Lapping 2005) and the amount of time that is given over to teaching–learning interactions. Equally, the types of spaces in which teaching–learning interactions take place can differ in relation to the position of a university in the field of higher education. For example, in their comparison of seminars in the discipline of English in different universities, Jones *et al.* (2005) and Bruce *et al.* (2007) argued that more 'elite' universities had more time and space in which to engage in teaching–learning interactions. These differences can again be seen to relate to institutions' positions in the field of higher education and the position of particular programmes within their particular institutional fields.

In this section I have tried to illustrate different ways in which institutional *habitus* can become situated within teaching–learning interactions. This has not intended to be an exhaustive examination of all the ways in which institutional *habitus* can become situated in teaching–learning interactions. Rather, I have tried to provide some illustrations of the ways in which institutions' position in the field of higher education will impact on their institutional *habitus* and the ways in which this *habitus* is subjected to change as it is refracted through the internal fields of a particular institution. These processes of refraction mean that the way in which institutional *habitus* shapes teaching–learning interactions cannot simply be read-off from an institution's position in the field of higher education. Equally, this focus on the way in which institutional *habitus* is refracted as it moves through the fields of particular institutions becomes even more important in the next section as I consider how teaching–learning interactions can be conceptualized from the viewpoint of institutional *habitus*.

Characterizing teaching–learning interactions in terms of institutional cultures

There are at least two reasons why it may seem a strange choice to draw on a Bourdieusian analysis to characterizing teaching–learning interactions from the perspective of institutional cultures. First, from Bourdieu's perspective it can appear that examining teaching–learning interactions in higher education in terms of teaching–learning processes is a *misrecognition* of its objective purpose. Bourdieu (1996) argues that this purpose is to transform social privilege into individual gifts, with education acting as the primary mechanism for transforming inherited capital into qualifications. Second, Bourdieu's approach is often criticized for making it difficult to get a sense of how to analyse the playing out of particular interactions (Mouzelis 2000; Mutch 2003; Naidoo 2004), the particular strategies that social agents adopt at a particular moment.

My focus on the way in which institutional *habitus* is refracted through the different internal fields of higher education institutions is crucial in responding to these criticisms. As I argued earlier, these fields may have different forms of symbolic capital at stake. Thus, in relation to the first issue of using Bourdieu's approach to conceptual-ize teaching–learning interactions, while at the level of the field of higher education what is at stake may be the conversion of social capital into qualifications (see Bourdieu and Passeron 1990; Bourdieu *et al.* 1994; Bourdieu 1996), once institutional *habitus* has been refracted through the different fields within an institution there might be different stakes in play. This means that different forms of symbolic capital can be at stake within different teaching–learning interactions. Thus I am suggesting that Bourdieu's account of *misrecognition* is only a problem when one attempts to relate the interaction of students and academics directly to the general field of higher education.

The criticisms that Bourdieu's approach cannot deal with the inter-actional strategies of academics and students is similarly based on attempts to directly relate the game of the field of higher education as a whole to these interactional strategies. Once account is taken of the ways in which institutional *habitus* is refracted through the different internal fields of an institution and the ways in which this changes the forms of capital at stake, then there is an opportunity to characterize teaching–learning interactions in terms of institutional cultures.

This characterization involves examining the different positions that students and academics take up in the field of the particular pro-gramme of study. In this way, teaching–learning interactions can be conceptualized as processes in which students and academics seek to maintain and develop the forms of capital that are at stake within that particular programme. There are two aspects to this. First, there is the field of the particular programme of study in which students and aca-demics are engaged. This informs the kinds of symbolic capital that are at stake within the programme of study. Second, there are the *habitus* of the academic and student within this field of the programme of study. It is important to recognize that, while such *habitus* will be related to those they hold in other fields, they may not be identical. Rather they will be the dispositions they have developed to deal with the regularities of this particular programme. As Bourdieu (2005) argues, these are not conscious dispositions but rather their views of what is reasonable for students and academics within this programme. So while, as Robbins (1993) and James (2000) argue, this is a matter of socialization, it is a socialization into a particular programme of study rather than into a particular institution as a whole.

So in terms of institutional cultures, teaching–learning interactions can be characterized as the interactions of the *habitus* of academics and students within the field of the programme of study. What forms of capital they seek to maintain and develop within these interactions is an empirical matter and will depend on the field of the particular programme and the *habitus* of the students and academics within the programme. However, as with the field of higher education more generally, it is likely that there will be a number of rival forms of symbolic capital that the different players will seek to establish as the most legitimate within that particular programme. This could include different types of knowledge (academic, vocational or social) that different students and academics emphasize in different ways. Again, it is important to emphasize that students and academics may not see their interactions within these terms but rather it is the focus of the research to understand the objective logic of the programme that leads them to seek to develop their capital in this way *and* to understand how the practices of students and academics lead them to act with unknown complicity within the game of the field.

The possibilities of a Bourdieusian analysis of the relations between institutional cultures and teaching–learning interactions

There are three possibilities of adopting the kind of Bourdieusian approach to analysing the relations between institutional cultures and teaching–learning interactions that I have developed in this chapter. First, in linking institutional *habitus* to a university's position in the wider field of higher education, it gives a sense of some of the origins of differences in institutional cultures in terms of differences in institutions' positions in the field of higher education. Second, in giving a sense of how institutional *habitus* is refracted through different fields within a particular institution, it gives a sense of how institutional cultures can play out differently in different parts of an institution and thus allows a way of accounting for intra-institutional differences. Thus institutional policies are refracted through the different fields of the institutions, such as faculties, departments and programmes of study, and take on different meanings depending on the forms of symbolic capital at stake within these fields. Third, in examining how the field of a particular programme is related to institutional *habitus*, it gives a sense of how institutional cultures impact on both academics and students within teaching–learning interactions.

Thus a Bourdieusian approach to analysing the relations between teaching–learning interactions and institutional cultures provides a range of tools with which to make a sense of the differences in the way that institutional cultures play out both within and between higher education institutions. While this chapter has examined some possible ways in which institutional *habitus* and teaching–learning interactions might relate, these tools need to be put to work in relation to empirical data to develop a sense of how these relations play out in different institutional cultures.

The tensions within a Bourdieusian analysis of the relations between institutional cultures and teaching–learning interactions

There are two main tensions with the approach that I have developed in this chapter to analysing the relations between institutional cultures and teaching–learning interactions. The first is related to the view of *habitus* that has underpinned my analysis. In arguing for the way in which institutional *habitus* is refracted through the different fields within an institution, I am very much seeing *habitus* as related to the particular field that students and academics are working within. This has a number of implications. It means that *habitus* is less of a synonym for a generic identity than is suggested in much research adopting a Bourdieusian approach (for example, see Reay 2004 for a discussion of its use in educational research) and more a way of understanding how students and academics respond to the games of very particular fields.

This tends to place Bourdieu's focus on the durability of the dispositions of the *habitus* into the background of the analysis and instead
foregrounds the ways in which these are refracted through a succession
of fields. While this approach can be supported by Bourdieu and
Waquant's (1992) insistence that field and *habitus* only operate in
relation to each other, it does raise the question of how much of the
notion of institutional cultures can be captured by the term institutional *habitus* and whether there are important aspects of institutional
cultures that are silenced by focusing on the way in which positions in
a number of inter- and intra-institutional fields shape institutional
habitus.

Second, in examining how institutional *habitus* is refracted through
a number of fields *within* institutions, it seems that I have moved away
from viewing institutional context as an interweaving and back towards
seeing these different fields as being *contained* within the institution
(see Chapter 2 for a discussion of Cole's 1996 use of this distinction).
This raises the question of whether these intra-institutional fields are
clearly distinguishable from each other in the way that I have implied.
Bourdieu and Waquant's (1992) view that the boundary of a field is
where its effects cease, seems to suggest that this is unlikely to be the
case. Thus the price of drawing on the notion of the field of the programme of study to get closer to the teaching–learning interaction
appears to be an awkward analytical separation of the different fields
within universities. I am not sure that there is an easy way of dealing
with this tension. Rather, it is something that needs to be examined in
relation to particular empirical examples and is another illustration of
the way in which different ways of conceptualizing teaching–learning
interactions have different possibilities and tensions associated with
their use.

Conclusion

In this chapter I have examined the potential of a Bourdieusian
analysis of the relations between teaching–learning interactions and
institutional cultures. I have argued that it overcomes a number of the
issues with Teaching and Learning Regimes as a way of understanding
this relationship. However, there are questions about its approach

including whether it offers a limited view of what is involved in institutional cultures and whether it limits the analytical power of the notions of field and *habitus*.

I have now examined the relations between teaching–learning interactions and teaching–learning environments, student and academic identities, disciplinary knowledge practices and institutional cultures. In the next chapter I bring my analyses in these different chapters together to examine the conceptual and methodological implications of the approaches to analysing teaching–learning interactions that I have considered in this book.

Chapter 8

Implications for researching teaching–learning interactions

Introduction

In this chapter I initially revisit the arguments that I developed in the previous chapters of this book and indicate the next steps I take in terms of examining their implications. This involves examining the conceptual and methodological implications of my arguments in relation to researching teaching–learning interactions in higher education. I draw these together by examining how they might inform future research in this area and conclude by returning to the complex and messy nature of teaching–learning interactions in higher education.

The story so far

My argument in this book is that there are two significant and related problems in drawing on the current literature on teaching–learning processes in higher education in order to examine teaching–learning interactions. First, the current literature tends to separate the experiences and practices of academics from those of students within teaching–learning processes. This has meant that this research does not support an examination of the dynamic and shifting aspects of teaching–learning interactions in higher education. Second, while there is a broad consensus in this literature about factors that shape teaching–learning processes in higher education, in terms of the teaching–learning environment, academics' and students' identities, disciplinary knowledge practices and institutional cultures, these sets of structural–agentic processes are often conceptualized as static containers of teaching–learning interactions rather than dynamic processes that are weaved into the very fabric of such interactions. These two issues are related because they both highlight a tendency to focus on teaching–learning interactions, and the processes that shape them, as in some way as fixed and regular rather than as emergent, contingent and unpredictable.

I argued that these shortcomings are directly related to the ways in which teaching–learning processes are conceptualized in this research. In order to examine this issue in more detail, in Chapter 2 I developed a conception of structure and agency that informed the rest of the book. I argued that the social world is complex and emergent, and as such the outcomes of social processes are contingent. In order to understand this complexity, I argued that researchers need to simplify the social world and that they do this through using theories. Different theories simplify the world in different ways, so in order to focus on the interactive and contingent aspects of such interactions requires simplifying conceptualizations that maintain a focus on these dynamic aspects of teaching–learning interactions. Based on this, I argued that there were two aspects that needed to be addressed in analysing the relations between sets of structural–agentic processes and teaching–learning interactions. First, it is necessary to analyse the ways in which sets of structural–agentic processes are situated in teaching–learning interactions. Second, it is necessary to characterize teaching–learning interactions in terms of the particular set of structural–agentic processes.

In Chapter 3, I outlined the shortcomings of the mainstream literature relating to teaching–learning processes in higher education in addressing these two aspects of analysing the relations between sets of structural–agentic processes and teaching–learning interactions. In particular I argued that the tendency in this research to foreground the perceptions or practices of academics or students in relation to teaching–learning processes means that it is difficult to gain a sense of how students and academics impact on each other in a dynamic and ongoing manner within particular teaching–learning interactions.

In Chapters 4 to 7, I examined four alternative ways of analysing the relations between sets of structural–agentic processes and teaching–learning interactions in higher education. Given the two aspects of such an analysis, this involved the examination of four ways in which sets of structural–agentic processes are situated in teaching–learning interactions and four ways in which teaching–learning interactions can be characterized in terms of structural–agentic processes.

In relation to the ways in which sets of structural–agentic processes are situated in teaching–learning interactions, there were four different accounts of the processes by which this occurs. In Chapter 4, I argued that from an Activity Theory perspective teaching–learning environments are situated in teaching–learning interactions in terms of the production of the interacting activity systems of academics and students who are engaged in teaching–learning interactions. In Chapter 5, I argued that a Symbolic Interactionist perspective suggests that student and academic identities are situated in teaching–learning interactions through the form of students' learning careers and the academics' teaching careers at a particular point in time. In Chapter 6, I argued that a Bernsteinian perspective highlights that situating disciplinary knowledge practices in teaching–learning interactions involves the transformation of such practices into curriculum. In Chapter 7, I argued that a Bourdieusian perspective foregrounds the ways in which institutional cultures are situated in teaching–learning interactions through the refraction of institutional *habitus* through the internal fields of particular higher education institutions. In each case, these perspectives highlighted the ways in which structural–agentic processes are changed as they are situated in teaching–learning interactions. Thus rather than being conceived as static containers of teaching–learning interactions, they are conceptualized as dynamic processes that are woven into the very fabric of teaching–learning interactions.

Over the course of Chapters 4 to 7, I also developed four characterizations of teaching–learning interactions in terms of sets of structural agentic processes. Drawing on Activity Theory in Chapter 4, I argued that teaching–learning interactions could be characterized, in terms of teaching–learning environments, as the interacting activity systems of academics and students. In Chapter 5, drawing on Symbolic Interactionism, I argued that in relation to student and academic identities, teaching–learning interactions could be characterized in terms of the shifting identity positions that are available to students and academics as they engage together. In Chapter 6, I argued that a Bernsteinian perspective supports a characterization of teaching–learning interactions in terms of disciplinary knowledge practices. This characterizes teaching–learning interactions as the relations between modes of pedagogic practice and the knowledge codes of students and academics. Drawing on a Bourdieusian perspective in Chapter 7, I argued that, in terms of institutional cultures, teaching–learning interaction can be characterized in terms of the relations between the different forms of symbolic capital maintained and developed by students and academics within the field of their programme of study. Each of these four characterizations maintains a sense of the different positions of students and academics within teaching–learning interactions, while also providing a way of thinking about how they impact on each other.

The next steps

In this chapter, I begin to draw together the different arguments in the preceding chapters in order to consider what implications they have as a whole for analysing teaching–learning interactions in higher education. I argue that there are two broad groups of implications: conceptual and methodological implications.

I first examine the conceptual implications of my approach. I argue that the major conceptual implication is that it is necessary to draw on different perspectives in order to understand different aspects of teaching–learning interactions in higher education. Thus rather than attempting to combine or synthesize different approaches with the aim of explaining *more*, the point is to understand that different perspectives explain *differently*. I then examine the methodological implications of the arguments that I have been developing in this book. I examine how my arguments relate to issues of how data are generated, analysed and their significance in relation to teaching–learning interactions in higher education.

In examining these different sets of implications I also want to show that these conceptual and methodological issues are closely related. Issues of how to think about the processes that are the subject of research are directly and intimately related to issues about how to generate and understand the significance of empirical data related to these processes. In examining these implications, I am not claiming that they are original in terms of conceptual and methodological literature relating to research in the social sciences more generally (for example, see Law 2004; Silverman 2006). However, I am arguing that they are issues that tend to be obscured in current research into teaching–learning processes in higher education. For this reason, I then examine how these implications might inform future research into teaching–learning interactions in higher education.

Conceptual implications

In examining the conceptual implications of my argument, I first expand in more detail on my argument about using a range of conceptual approaches to analyse the complexity of teaching–learning interactions. This is not an argument that any theory is as good as another in seeking to conceptualize such interactions, and so, in developing this argument, I also consider some criteria for deciding which theories might be 'more helpful' in conceptualizing particular aspects of teaching–learning interactions.

I have argued throughout this book that, in attempting to understand the complexity of teaching–learning interactions, it is necessary to draw on a range of conceptual perspectives to analyse different aspects of such interactions. It is important to be clear that it is not an argument that a way should be found to *combine or synthesize* the insights of the different perspectives into a single approach that is capable of accounting for all of the different processes that come together in particular teaching–learning interactions. This would be to oversimplify a complex interaction. Rather, my argument is that different ways of conceptualizing teaching–learning interactions can provide ways of explaining them *differently* (for a similar analysis of the shifting 'theory narratives' of the relations between learning, work and education see Saunders 2006). This is because, rather than these different ways of analysing teaching–learning interactions being independent, they overlap in different ways. Thus each of the perspectives that I have examined draws the threads of teaching–learning interactions together in different ways. Some elements of these threads may be common to different perspectives but the way they are combined with other threads will be different. Thus drawing on Bourdieu to analyse the relations between institutional cultures and teaching–learning interactions included common elements to a Bernsteinian analysis of the relations between disciplinary knowledge practices and teaching–learning interactions. However, in each analysis these elements were combined in different ways with elements that were not common to both approaches.

As with the structural–agentic processes I have examined in this book, the conceptual perspectives I have analysed are not intended to be exhaustive. The whole point of the argument in this book is that more ways are needed of conceptualizing teaching–learning interactions in higher education. There are other approaches that I could have equally examined. For example, Haggis (2006) argues that complexity theory offers a useful way of understanding students as 'dynamic systems' and how their histories and different aspects of their lives impact on the narratives of their experiences in higher education, while Ollin (2008) draws on the notion of 'figured worlds' (Holland *et al.* 1998) to examine the significance of silence in teaching–learning interactions. However, the point is that no single approach can deal with all of the complexity of teaching–learning processes: some are more useful for asking some questions than others because they foreground and background different aspects of teaching–learning processes. Thus Haggis (2006, p. 12) argues that within her approach, 'learning . . . seemed to disappear as any kind of recognizable generic entity'. My argument is that such disappearances are the result of the simplifications that are attendant on using any conceptual framework rather than necessarily reflecting a deeper reality.

This does not mean that different conceptual approaches cannot be brought together in order to provide a new way of conceptualizing teaching–learning interactions. Rather, it is to emphasize two aspects of such attempts to bring different conceptual approaches together. First, this is a significant piece of conceptual work in itself and not something that can be achieved quickly or easily. Second, rather than explaining more, the resulting conceptual approach is again likely to explain *differently*. This is because in order to understand the empirical world it has to be simplified through concepts and, as I have argued many times, different theories simplify in different ways. Thus, as Mol and Law (2002) argue, the issue is to be sensitive to the simplifications that particular conceptual approaches involve and to question the work that such simplifications do in shaping the research process and outcomes. This also means that siren cries of 'overcoming dualisms' (for example, see Hodkinson *et al.* 2008) are, in fact, likely to lead to other dualisms or simplifications. In this way I am arguing that the reason dualisms are so common in research is because they are a result of the necessity of simplifying the social world in order to analyse it. Clearly it is possible to argue over which dualisms are the most pernicious and to attempt to think in terms of spectra rather than dualities but I think it is disingenuous to suggest that there are dualism-free ways of understanding the social world readily at hand.

This should not to be taken to imply that I am arguing that, in choosing a perspective to analyse teaching–learning interactions in higher education, 'anything goes'. As I have shown in previous chapters, different ways are needed to analyse different aspects of the factors that come together in teaching–learning interactions. Some ways of analysing particular aspects of teaching–learning interactions are more helpful than others. Clearly, a lot is at stake in determining what counts as 'more helpful'. For this reason, I want to outline three aspects of 'more helpful' that informed the choice of conceptual perspectives that I have examined in this book.

The internal consistency of the conceptual perspective

The first aspect is the internal consistency of the conceptual perspective. This is particularly an issue when trying to bring different conceptual perspectives together. All of the perspectives that I explored were chosen because they appeared to offer consistency in the way that they conceptualized different aspects of teaching–learning interactions. Clearly, this does not mean that they were not without their problems. For each perspective I identified tensions in the way that I had drawn on them to analyse teaching–learning interactions. It is also important to be clear that in each case, although to differing extents, my use of each approach to analyse teaching–learning interactions in higher education represented, in Bernstein's (2000) terms, a process of 'recontextualization'. Thus in each case I adapted the theory to the context of teaching–learning interactions. In some cases, as with Symbolic Interactionism, this adaptation was minimal, but in others it was more involved, for example in using Bourdieu to examine the relations between institutional cultures and teaching–learning interactions. In each case, to maintain the internal consistency of the approach, I tried to do this by thinking about how to apply the perspectives to teaching–learning interactions in their own terms rather than adding conceptual tools from other perspectives.

The appropriateness of the perspective for analysing particular aspects of teaching–learning interactions

The second aspect is the appropriateness of a perspective to deal with the particular questions raised by examining the particular aspect of teaching–learning interactions. There were two elements of this aspect of the choice of conceptual perspectives in the book. The first was characterized in my consideration of the relative strengths of the current ways of analysing particular aspects of teaching–learning inter- actions in Chapter 3 and the alternatives that I examined in Chapters 4 to 7. Again my argument was that the different perspectives high- lighted different aspects of teaching–learning processes in higher education and that the alternatives I considered might be more helpful in thinking about the relations between particular structural–agentic processes and teaching–learning interactions. This does not mean that I am suggesting that the approaches I considered in Chapter 3 should be abandoned. Rather, my point was that, while each of these ap- proaches has been helpful in thinking about the perceptions and practices of students and academics, they have not been as helpful in thinking about the interactive aspects of teaching–learning processes in higher education.

The second aspect of this choice process was related to which of the alternative approaches were most useful for examining the relations between particular sets of structural–agentic processes and teaching– learning interactions. Again, some choices were straightforward, such as using Symbolic Interactionism to examine the relations between student and academic identities and teaching–learning interactions, as examining such relations is an underlying focus of Symbolic Inter- actionism. In other cases the choice was more involved. For example, Bernstein and Bourdieu both offer analyses of disciplinary knowledge practices and institutional cultures in their work. My choice was based on the judgement that a Bernsteinian persepective highlighted the transformation of disciplinary knowledge practices into curriculum, while Bourdieu's concept of the field of higher education highlighted aspects of the origins of institutional cultures. However, it seems likely that for others the opposite judgement might make more sense. In this way the choice of a particular perspective is not a once-and-for-all affair but something that needs to be revisited through an examination of the relations between the perspective and empirical data relating to the relations between the particular set of structural–agentic processes and teaching–learning interactions.

The relationship between the conceptual perspective and empirical data

This brings me to the third element in the choice of perspectives for analysing the relations between structural–agentic processes and teaching–learning interactions. This is concerned with thinking about the relationship between the different perspectives and empirical data. There are two aspects to this relationship. First, ensuring that the theory does not structure the research so much that the outcomes of the research are simply a tautological restating of the theory (see Ashwin 2008 for a further discussion of this) but, second, making sure that the theory does enough work in informing the conceptualization of the research in terms of helping to frame the approach to developing the research questions, the approach to data analysis and understanding the significance of the outcomes of the research. This is an important issue because in arguing that there is a complex and emergent social world out there, which can only be accessed through simplifying theories, implies that it is crucial to examine the relationship between theories and their empirical instantiations. To put this another way, because conceptual frameworks constitute the research object and they inform researchers what the research object is like, it is essential that the empirical world has the space to knock against these conceptions so that any lack of fit is made visible rather than obscured.

All of the perspectives that I examined in Chapters 4 to 7 explicitly discuss this relationship and offer the space for empirical data to develop the conceptual resources. Indeed, this is a central issue in the literatures of each of the perspectives that I examined. Thus I discussed Activity Theory's focus on generating views of particular activity systems, Blumer's (1969) argument for 'sensitizing concepts' in relation to Symbolic Interactionism, and Bourdieu's focus on examining empirical examples of the concepts of 'field', 'capital' and '*habitus*'. It is something that Bernstein (2000) discusses in some detail in terms of 'languages of description' (see also Brown 2006; Moore 2006).

Bernstein (2000) argues that a theory has an 'internal' and an 'external' language of description. The internal language of description is the way in which the theory simplifies the social world; that is, the assumptions that the theory makes about the social world, the sorts of phenomena that it foregrounds and the relations between these phenomena. The external language of description describes what would count as an empirical substantiation of the theory. Bernstein (2000) is clear that this must be done in a non-circular way, that there must be space for the empirical world to offer a contradiction of the theory. For this reason Brown (2006, p. 144) argues that the notion of Languages of Description:

> establishes a dynamic relationship between theory, empirical research, and practice, and fosters an openness and transparency in presentation of the analysis of data that facilitates both induction into the practices of analysis and critical engagement with processes and products of research.

Thus any theory needs to be capable of being developed by the empirical data that are generated; otherwise the danger is that any empirical data can be seen as supporting the theory (see Dowling 1998 for a further discussion of languages of description).

That research into teaching–learning processes in higher education struggles with the relationship between conceptual perspectives and empirical data is illustrated by Tight's (2004) analysis of research into 'teaching and learning', 'course design' and 'student experience' in higher education journals outside of North America in 2000. This analysis suggested that only about one-third of the studies showed any engagement with theoretical resources. Often those that use theoretical resources do not seem to result in analyses of how the theory has been developed in the relationship with empirical data but rather offer the theoretical approach as a way of explaining the data. Thus the analysis of data is used to illustrate the theory rather than to challenge and develop it. This is not to suggest that developing theory through its relationship with empirical data is easy; it is difficult and time-consuming, but if theories are to be developed further, there is a need to think seriously about this relationship.

In summary, then, my argument is that the conceptual perspectives that are most helpful in analysing teaching–learning interactions in higher education are those that have an internal consistency, that are appropriate for analysing the particular aspect of teaching–learning interactions that are under consideration and that provide space for empirical data to develop the conceptual approach while also providing sufficient resources to frame the research. In the next section I move on to consider the methodological implications of the approach that I have developed in this book.

Methodological implications

As well as having a number of conceptual implications, my argument in this book also has a number of methodological implications. These are a development of where I ended up in considering the conceptual implications of my argument. Thus I begin this section by again briefly examining the relationship between conceptual perspectives and generating data about teaching–learning interactions. In this case I focus on how the conceptual approach informs the way in which data are generated, analysed and their significance argued for. In doing so I focus on the implications of two related aspects of my argument: that it is researchers who constitute the object of their research, and the importance of using conceptual frameworks in a way that allows empirical data the space to challenge them. As with the conceptual implications, I am not claiming that these are original in relation to understandings of research within the social sciences more generally (again see Law 2004); rather, my argument is that they do not appear to inform a significant amount of research into teaching–learning processes in higher education. In the previous section I argued that conceptual perspectives need to do enough work in informing the way in which research questions, research methods and approaches to data analysis were developed in particular studies. I now want to consider this aspect of 'more helpful' in more detail.

Generating data about teaching–learning interactions

As I have argued, the conceptual perspectives that are used to analyse teaching–learning interactions play a major role in constituting the object of research. They do this by characterizing the sorts of processes that are under consideration and the limits of the teaching–learning interaction. As Law (1994, p. 194) argues, such processes are not 'given in the order of things' but rather constituted by ways of ordering the world (what I have called 'conceptual perspectives'). Thus different conceptual perspectives will 'create' different research objects. My criticism of Approaches to Learning and Teaching and Social Practices in relation to thinking about teaching–learning interactions in higher education is that the research objects they constitute (perceptions and practices respectively) are not helpful in thinking about the interactive aspects of teaching–learning processes. As well as being a conceptual problem, it is important to be clear that this is a methodological problem. It is a problem with the tools that are available to generate data about teaching–learning interactions.

The problem is this: the vast majority of studies of teaching–learning processes in higher education are based on data generated solely from the accounts of academics and students, usually through interviews or questionnaires or through a mixture of the two. Evidence for this comes from Tight's (2003) analysis of the methods used in research of 'teaching and learning', 'course design' and 'student experience' published in higher education journals outside of North America in the year 2000. This is a problem for two reasons. First, these accounts are usually generated outside of teaching–learning interactions and so tend to lose a sense of the different positions that students and academics might move through in a particular interaction. In this way the dynamic, contingent aspects of such interactions and the sense that things could have turned out differently are lost. Second, in trying to get a sense of the relations between sets of structural–agentic processes and teaching–learning interactions, it is clear that students and academics are not always aware of these relations and how they impact on their experience of these interactions. This raises issues about what status can be given to their accounts when researching teaching–learning interactions.

It is important to be clear that I am not suggesting that there are simple methodological solutions to these issues. Chapters 4 to 7 all emphasize, albeit in different ways, that the meaning that students and academics attribute to such interactions are key to the way in which they conduct themselves within those interactions. This means that the observation of teaching–learning interactions, on its own, will not resolve this issue. Equally, approaches such as 'dialogic interviewing' (Knight and Saunders 1999) may help academics and students to reflect on structural–agentic processes but it will not help to capture the interactive aspects of teaching–learning processes. Other approaches such as asking academics and students to reflect on videos of teaching–learning interactions in which they were involved offer some interesting possibilities (for example, see Mann 2003; Jones *et al.* 2005). However, these approaches have their own associated problems such as the sheer amount of data that they tend to produce. The point then is not to suggest that there are easy solutions but rather to suggest that generating data about teaching–learning interactions is a problematic and messy exercise. As such, there is a need to be careful and, in Law's (1994) terms, 'modest' about what is claimed on the basis of such data.

Analysing data about teaching–learning interactions in higher education

As I argued in relation to its conceptual implications, my argument highlights the importance of conceptual perspectives providing the space for empirical data to develop them. This means ensuring that the empirical data do more than simply illustrate the conceptual perspective but actually have the space to challenge its assumptions. The analysis of empirical data is crucial in this. Sometimes the analysis of, for example, interview data relating to teaching–learning processes in higher education can appear to be little more than the identification of 'juicy' quotations that are argued to illustrate the analysis that has been developed. There is little sense given of how particular quotations relate to the data set as whole, for example how common this type of observation was from the participants in the research. The problem with this is that different conceptual perspectives highlight different kinds of quotations. This means that, without a sense of how the individual quotation relates to the overall structure of the data, it is quite possible that the quotations selected simply reflect the conceptual perspective adopted rather than saying anything about the data which have been generated. This is one way in which research can become tautological.

One implication of this argument is that it questions the notion that research can unproblematically 'give a voice' to students or academics and instead suggests that it obscures the role researchers play in selecting and analysing data when they claim they are reflecting the thoughts of those they research (for a fascinating discussion of the relations between 'voice discourses' and theories of knowledge see Moore and Muller 1999; Young 2008).

Again, this is not to suggest that there are easy alternatives or that those who take this approach are deliberately trying to mislead or engage in special pleading for their conceptual perspective. Rather, it is to suggest that the way in which data is reduced from, for example, pages and pages of transcripts to a small number of quotations in a paper plays a crucial role in shaping the research outcomes. If this is done with the intention to confirm rather than to challenge the conceptual perspective underpinning the research, then it is highly likely that there will be little or no space for the empirical data to challenge particular aspects of that conceptual perspective.

While I have used data generated through interviews as an example to illustrate this argument, it should not be assumed that this is simply a problem with qualitative research into teaching–learning processes in higher education. There are similar problems with quantitative research. For example, in relation to the claims made on the basis of questionnaire data, there can be a tendency to suggest that the constructs measured by questionnaires exist in the real world rather than being 'produced' by the items and scales that make up the particular inventory. Equally, some of the claims based on the use of these questionnaires seem to forget that the origins of these data are academics and students responding to a particular set of questions at a particular time.

Again, this is not to suggest that the analyses of such studies are flawed or there are easy ways of avoiding such issues. Rather, it is to argue for modesty in reporting these outcomes and to argue for more discussion of the difficult choices that are made in both qualitative and quantitative data analysis. This includes careful discussion of the problematic issue of what the analysed data represent, for example how much they reflect the ways in which they were generated and analysed, and how much they reflect the ways in which academics and students engage in teaching–learning interactions in higher education. Equally, it is fairly obvious that it is not possible to report all aspects of the research process, but there is a need to pay attention to what is 'deleted' (Law 1994) in such accounts and what work is done by such deletions. My argument is that the current way in which much of the process of data analysis is deleted within accounts of research into teaching–learning processes in higher education conceals much of the work that researchers have done to generate their research outcomes and makes it more difficult for the analysed empirical data to challenge the conceptual perspectives, whether implicit or explicit, that underpin the design of the study.

The significance of the research outcomes

In thinking about what is deleted within accounts of the research process, another aspect is how the position of the researcher impacts on the outcomes of research. This aspect points to the need for reflexivity within the research process, but a particular type of reflexivity. As Bourdieu (2000) argues, this is not about reflecting on how the biography of an individual impacts on the research, but thinking about how the position of researchers within their academic field might impact on their research. For Bourdieu, academic research is a social practice that takes place in a field. Therefore, researchers' investments in the games at stake in the field are likely to impact on their research. This means that researchers need to consider how their position in this field impacts on research by finding the filters that alter their perception of the phenomena that they are researching.

For Bourdieu, this reflexivity is a collective, rather than an individual activity (see Bourdieu and Waquant 1992; Bourdieu 2000). Thus it is for the research community as a whole to think about how the field of their research impacts on the outcomes of the research that they are involved in. *Homo Academicus* (Bourdieu 1988) is partly an example of Bourdieu's form of reflexivity in that he turns his analysis onto his own field, and his own position is included in his analysis of the forms of capital held by named Parisian academics. Such forms of collective reflexivity would involve discussions of how particular conceptual frameworks and methodological approaches lead some aspects of processes to be highlighted and not others. In this way, this book can be seen as an attempt to promote such reflexive discussions.

This is related to the significance of research outcomes because it emphasizes the incompleteness of any explanations of aspects of teaching–learning interactions in higher education. This is for a number of reasons. First, any such explanations are incomplete because there will always be another way of conceptualizing them that foregrounds different aspects of such interactions. Second, the research process itself is always to some extent provisional and incomplete. Thus the way in which data are analysed at one moment may be subject to change as researchers develop an understanding of their conceptual perspectives, the interactions they are analysing, and their position within the research field. Thus all research outcomes reflect where the researchers stand at a particular moment in time. Bourdieu (2004) highlighted the 'scholastic tendency' to describe science as something that is complete rather than something that it is the process of being made. It is to avoid this tendency that Law (1998) argues for a modest approach to research that acknowledges the incompleteness of research, and exposes the contingent and uncertain elements of the claims that are made on the basis of such research.

Future research into teaching–learning interactions in higher education

I now want to draw these implications together to consider how they might inform future research into teaching–learning interactions in higher education. First, as I have stressed throughout this book, what is required are more empirical studies that are focused on examining the relations between particular sets of structural–agentic processes and teaching–learning interactions. Such projects need to be framed by an explicit conceptual framework and designed in a way that provides the space for the empirical data to interrogate the conceptual framework. The ways of generating and analysing data need to be informed by the conceptual approach, and researchers need to consider how the conceptual approach and methods of data generation and analysis have shaped the outcomes of the research. In doing so, the unfinished aspects of all analyses of teaching–learning interactions need to be recognized.

As I have argued, these are difficult issues to address. For example, generating data that reflects the dynamic and shifting aspects of teaching–learning interactions is difficult and the analysis of these data is not straightforward. Given these difficulties, these are not issues that can be resolved in single research projects. They can only be addressed by a wide range of researchers engaging in a wide range of research projects in relation to teaching–learning interactions in higher education. Therefore, as with reflexivity, this is something that needs to be addressed collectively rather than individually. Such collectivity would involve an openness about the difficulties involved in researching teaching–learning interactions in higher education, a modesty about what can be achieved in single projects, and an understanding that a variety of perspectives is needed to understand the different aspects of teaching–learning interactions rather than sterile arguments about the misguided nature of different perspectives. Given perceived pressures from policymakers and funders for unambiguous answers to simple questions and the pressing demands of day-to-day educational practice, an argument for such collectivity may appear naïve earnestness *in extremis*. However, I am not sure that there is another way to develop a deeper understanding of the dynamic and shifting aspects of teaching–learning interactions and the ways in which they are shaped by structural–agentic processes.

Concluding thoughts

This book has been an attempt to think about how to analyse teaching–learning interactions in higher education, to think about the ways in which such interactions can be conceptualized, and the ways in which different perspectives foreground and background different aspects of such interactions. In this final chapter I have attempted to illustrate some of the implications of this attempt both for the ways in which teaching–learning interactions are conceptualized and the ways in which empirical data are generated and analysed in relation to such interactions. In concluding this book I want to highlight the two-way relations between conceptual perspectives and empirical data.

As I have argued, space needs to be given for empirical data to knock against conceptual perspectives and change them. This includes the possibility that a particular perspective might be rejected as a helpful way of understanding particular aspects of teaching–learning interactions. The implication of this is that conceptual frameworks themselves are always provisional, thus the development of a conceptual framework for analysing teaching–learning interactions is not a 'once-and-for-all' affair but something that is returned to within and between research projects. One way of interpreting my argument in this book would be, 'First, get your framework and then use that to generate and analyse data about a particular aspect of teaching–learning interactions.' The point that I want to make is that research is not like this in practice. Sometimes within a project, you can realize you have actually done something different from what you thought you were doing or that your analysis of the data is shifting your understanding and you need another framework to think about it. This is exactly what research should do; otherwise there would be no need to generate any data. My argument is that while these are essential parts of the research process, it is important to think through how they impact on research outcomes.

It is the complex, messy, unfinished nature of analysing teaching–learning interactions that I want to finish by emphasizing. While all conceptual frameworks simplify the complex nature of teaching–learning interactions, it is essential to come back to thinking about their complexity, for, as McKeachie (1974) eloquently argued, it is in their interactive, challenging complexity that their humanity lies.

References

Abbas, A. and McLean, M. (2007a) Qualitative research as a method for making just comparisons of pedagogic quality in higher education: a pilot study. *British Journal of Sociology of Education*, 28, 6: 723–37.

—— (2007b) Tackling inequality through quality: a comparative case study exploring university sociology lecturers' views using Bernsteinian concepts. Paper presented at *Learning Together: Reshaping Higher Education in a Global Age*, Institute of Education, University of London, 22–24 July 2007.

Ahearn, A., Broadbent, O., Collins, J. and Spentza, E. (2008) Being an undergraduate student in the twenty-first century. In R. Barnett and R. Di Napoli (eds) (2008) *Changing Identities in Higher Education: Voicing Perspectives*. London: Routledge.

Åkerlind, G. (2003) Growing and developing as a university teacher: variation in meaning. *Studies in Higher Education*, 28, 4: 375–90.

—— (2005) Variation and commonality in phenomenographic research methods. *Higher Education Research and Development*, 24: 321–34.

—— (2007) Constraints on academics' potential for developing as a teacher. *Studies in Higher Education*, 32, 1: 21–37.

Åkerlind, G. and Kayrooz, C. (2003) Understanding academic freedom: the views of social scientists. *Higher Education Research and Development*, 22: 327–44.

Alvesson, M. (2002) *Understanding Organizational Culture*. London: Sage Publications.

Anderson, C. and Day, K. (2005) Purposive environments: engaging students in the values and practices of history. *Higher Education*, 49: 319–43.

Anderson, C. and Hounsell, D. (2007) Knowledge practices: 'doing the subject' in undergraduate courses. *The Curriculum Journal*, 18: 463–78.

Anderson, P. and Williams, J. (eds) (2001) *Identity and Difference in Higher Education: 'Outsiders Within'*. Aldershot: Ashgate.

Apple, M. (1979) *Ideology and Curriculum*. London: Routledge and Kegan Paul.

Archer, L. (2003) The value of higher education. In L. Archer, M. Hutchings and A. Ross (eds) *Higher Education and Social Class: Issues of Exclusion and Inclusion*. London: RoutledgeFalmer.

—— (2006) Round pegs into square holes? Critical issues for the widening participation agenda. In D. Jary and R. Jones (eds) *Perspectives in Widening Participation in the Social Sciences*. Birmingham: Sociology, Anthropology, Politics (C-SAP), The Higher Education Academy Network.

—— (2008a) The new neoliberal subjects? Young/er academics' constructions of professional identity. *Journal of Education Policy*, 23, 3: 265–85.

—— (2008b) Younger academics' constructions of 'authenticity', 'success' and professional identity. *Studies in Higher Education*, 33, 4: 385–403.

Archer, L. and Leathwood, C. (2003) Identities, inequalities and higher education. In L. Archer, M. Hutchings and A. Ross (eds) *Higher Education and Social Class: Issues of Exclusion and Inclusion*. London: RoutledgeFalmer.

Archer, M. (1995) *Realist Social Theory: The Morphogenetic Approach*. Cambridge: Cambridge University Press.

—— (2003) *Structure, Agency and the Internal Conversation*. Cambridge: Cambridge University Press.

Arnot, M. and Reay, D. (2004) The framing of pedagogic encounters: regulating the social order in classroom learning. In J. Muller, B. Davies and A. Morais (eds) *Reading Bernstein, Researching Bernstein*. London: RoutledgeFalmer.

Ashwin, P. (2003a) Peer facilitation and how it contributes to the development of a more social view of learning. *Research in Post-Compulsory Education*, 8: 5–17.

—— (2003b) Peer support: relations between the context, process and outcomes for the students who are supported. *Instructional Science*, 31: 159–73.

—— (2005) Variation in students' experiences of the Oxford tutorial. *Higher Education*, 50: 631–44.

—— (ed.) (2006a) *Changing Higher Education: The Development of Learning and Teaching*. London: Routledge.

—— (2006b) Variation in academics' accounts of tutorials. *Studies in Higher Education*, 31: 651–65.

—— (2008) Accounting for structure and agency in close-up research on teaching, learning and assessment in higher education. *International Journal of Educational Research*, 47, 3: 151–8.

Ashwin, P. and McLean, M. (2005) Towards a reconciliation of the approaches to learning and critical pedagogy perspectives in higher education through a focus on academic engagement. In C. Rust (ed.) *Improving Student Learning 12: Diversity and Inclusivity*. Oxford: Oxford Centre for Staff and Learning Development.

Ashworth, P. (2004) Developing useable pedagogic research skills. In Rust C. (ed.) *Improving Student Learning: Theory Research and Scholarship*. Oxford: Oxford Centre for Staff and Learning Development.

Atkinson, P. (1997) *The Clinical Experience: The Construction and Reconstruction of Medical Reality*. Second Edition. Aldershot: Ashgate.

Atkinson, P. and Housley, W. (2003) *Interactionism: An Essay in Sociological Amnesia*. London: Sage Publications.

Barab, S., Barnett, M., Yamagata-Lynch, L., Squire, K. and Keating, T. (2002) Using Activity Theory to understand the systemic tensions characterising a technology rich introductory astronomy course. *Mind, Culture, and Activity*, 9, 2: 76–107.

Barnett, R. and Di Napoli, R. (eds) (2008) *Changing Identities in Higher Education: Voicing Perspectives*. London: Routledge.

Barton, D. (2007) *Literacy: An Introduction to the Ecology of Written Language*. Second Edition. Oxford: Blackwell Publishing.

Barton, D. and Hamilton, M. (1998) *Local Literacies: Reading and Writing in One Community*. London: Routledge.

—— (2005) Literacy, reification and the dynamics of social interaction. In D. Barton and K. Tursting (eds) *Beyond Communities of Practice: Language, Power and Social Context*. Cambridge: Cambridge University Press.

Barton, D. and Tursting, K. (eds) (2005) *Beyond Communities of Practice: Language, Power and Social Context*. Cambridge: Cambridge University Press.

Bathmaker, A-M., Brooks, G., Parry, G. and Smith, D. (2008) Dual-sector further and higher education: policies, organisations and students in transition. *Research Papers in Education*, 23, 2: 125–37.

Baynham, M. (1995) *Literacy Practices: Investigating Literacy in Social Contexts*. London: Longman.

Becher, T. (1989) *Academic Tribes and Territories: Intellectual Enquiry and the Cultures of*

Disciplines. Buckingham: Society for Research into Higher Education and Open University Press.

Becher, T. and Parry, S. (2005) The endurance of disciplines. In I. Bleiklie and M. Henkel (eds) *Governing Knowledge: A Study of Continuity and Change in Higher Education*. Dordrecht: Springer.

Becher, T. and Trowler, P. (2001) *Academic Tribes and Territories: Intellectual Enquiry and the Cultures of Disciplines*. Second Edition. Buckingham: Society for Research into Higher Education and Open University Press.

Beck, J. (2002) The sacred and the profane in recent struggles to promote official pedagogic identities. *British Journal of Sociology of Education*, 23, 4: 617–26.

Beck, J. and Young, M. (2005) The assault on the professions and the restructuring of academic and professional identities: a Bernsteinian analysis. *British Journal of Sociology of Education*, 26, 2: 183–97.

Becker, H. (1963) *Outsiders: Studies in the Sociology of Deviance*. New York: The Free Press.

Becker, H., Geer, B. and Hughes, E. (1968) *Making the Grade: The Academic Side of College Life*. Chicago: University of Chicago Press.

Becker, H., Geer, B., Hughes, E. and Strauss, A. (1961) *Boys in White*. Chicago: University of Chicago Press.

Berglund, A. (2004) A framework to study learning in a complex learning environment. *ALT-J*, 12, 1: 65–79.

Bernstein, B. (1975) *Class Codes and Control Volume 3: Towards a Theory of Educational Transmissions*. Second Edition. London: Routledge and Kegan Paul.

—— (1990) *The Structuring of Pedagogic Discourse: Volume IV Class, Codes and Control*. London: Routledge.

—— (2000) *Pedagogy, Symbolic Control and Identity: Theory, Research and Critique*. Revised Edition. Oxford: Rowman and Littlefield Publishers.

—— (2001) From pedagogies to knowledges. In A. Morais, I. Neves, B. Davies and H. Daniels (eds) *Towards a Sociology of Pedagogy: The Contribution of Basil Bernstein to Research*. New York: Peter Lang.

Bhopal, K. (2002) Teaching women's studies: the effects of 'race' and gender. *Journal of Further and Higher Education*, 26, 2: 109–18.

Biggs, J. (1979) Individual differences in study processes and the quality of learning outcomes. *Higher Education*, 8: 381–94.

—— (1993) From theory to practice: a cognitive systems approach. *Higher Education Research and Development*, 12: 73–85

Bloomer, M. (1997) *Curriculum Making in Post-16 Education: The Social Conditions of Studentship*. London: Routledge.

—— (2001) Young lives, learning and transformation: some theoretical considerations. *Oxford Review of Education*, 27, 1: 429–49.

Bloomer, M. and Hodkinson, P. (1997) *Moving into Further Education: The Voice of the Learner*. London: Further Education Development Agency.

—— (1999) *College Life: The Voice of the Learner*. London: Further Education Development Agency.

—— (2000) Learning careers: continuity and change in young people's dispositions to learning. *British Educational Research Journal*, 26, 5: 583–97.

Blumer, H. (1969) *Symbolic Interactionism: Perspective and Method*. Berkeley: University of California Press.

Bourdieu, P. (1977) *Outline of a Theory of Practice*. Translated by R. Nice. Cambridge: Cambridge University Press.

—— (1988) *Homo Academicus*. Translated by P. Collier. Cambridge: Polity Press.

—— (1990a) *The Logic of Practice*. Translated by R. Nice. Cambridge: Polity Press.

—— (1990b) *In Other Words: Essays Towards a Reflexive Sociology*. Translated by M. Adamson. Cambridge: Polity Press.

—— (1993) *The Field of Cultural Production*. Cambridge: Polity Press.

—— (1996) *The State Nobility: Elite Schools in the Field of Power*. Translated by L. Clough. Cambridge: Polity Press.

—— (2000) *Pascalian Meditations*. Translated by R. Nice. Cambridge: Polity Press

—— (2004) *Science of Science and Reflexivity*. Translated by R. Nice. Cambridge: Polity Press.

—— (2005) *The Social Structures of the Economy*. Translated by C. Turner. Cambridge: Polity Press.

Bourdieu, P. and Passeron, J-C. (1979) *The Inheritors. French Students and their Relation to Culture*. Translated by R. Nice. Chicago: University of Chicago Press.

—— (1990) *Reproduction in Education, Society and Culture*. Translated by R. Nice. Second Edition. London: Sage Publications.

Bourdieu, P. and Wacquant, L. (1992) *An Invitation to Reflexive Sociology*. Cambridge: Polity Press.

Bourdieu, P., Passeron. J-C. and de Saint Martin, M. (1994) *Academic Discourse*. Translated by R. Teese. Cambridge: Polity Press.

Brennan, J. and Jary, D. (2005) What is learned at university? *The Social and Organisational Mediation of University Learning (SOMUL): Working Paper 1*. York: Higher Education Academy.

Brennan, J. and Naidoo, R. (2008) Higher education and the achievement (and/or prevention) of equity and social justice. *Higher Education*, 56: 287–302.

Brennan, J. and Osborne, M. (2005a) The organisational mediation of university learning. *The Social and Organisational Mediation of University Learning (SOMUL): Working Paper 2*. York: Higher Education Academy.

—— (2005b) Organisational mediation and higher education diversity. Teaching and Learning Research Project Annual Conference, University of Warwick.

—— (2008) Higher education's many diversities: of students, institutions and experiences; and outcomes? *Research Papers in Education*, 23, 2: 179–90.

Brew, A. (2006) *Research and Teaching: Beyond the Divide*. Basingstoke: Palgrave MacMillan.

—— (2008) Disciplinary and interdisciplinary affiliations of experienced researchers. *Higher Education*, 56: 423–38.

Brint, S., Cantwell, A.and Hanneman, R. (2008) The two cultures of undergraduate engagement. *Research in Higher Education*, 49: 383–402.

Brooks, R. (2006) Young graduates and lifelong learning: the impact of institutional stratification. *Sociology*, 40, 6: 1019–37.

Brooks, R. and Everett, G. (2008a) The impact of higher education on lifelong learning. *International Journal of Lifelong Education*, 27, 3: 239–54.

—— (2008b) The prevalence of 'life planning': evidence from UK graduates. *British Journal of Sociology of Education*, 29, 3: 325–37.

Brown, A. (2006) Languages of description and the education of researchers. In R. Moore, M. Arnot, J. Beck and H. Daniels (eds) *Knowledge, Power and Educational Reform: Applying the Sociology of Basil Bernstein*. London: Routledge.

Brown, J. and Duguid, P. (1991) Organizational Learning and Communities of Practice: toward a unified view of working, learning and innovating. *Organization Science*, 2, 1: 40–57.

Bruce, S., Jones, K. and McLean, M. (2007) Some notes on a project: democracy and authority in the production of a discipline. *Pedagogy*, 7: 481–500.

Bufton, S. (2006) Learning to play the game: mature, working-class students in higher education. In D. Jary and R. Jones (eds) *Perspectives in Widening Participation in the Social Sciences*. Birmingham: Sociology, Anthropology, Politics (C-SAP), The Higher Education Academy Network.

Byrne, D. (1998) *Complexity Theory and the Social Sciences*. London: Routledge.

Callender, C. (2008) The impact of term-time employment on higher education students' academic attainment and achievement. *Journal of Education Policy*, 23, 4: 359–77.

Callender, C. and Jackson, J. (2008) Does the fear of debt constrain choice of university and subject of study? *Studies in Higher Education*, 33, 4: 405–29.

Case, J. (2008) Alienation and engagement: development of an alternative theoretical framework for understanding student learning. *Higher Education*, 55: 321–32.

Cassidy, C. and Trew, K. (2001) Assessing identity change: a longitudinal study of the transition from school to college. *Group Processes and Intergroup Relations*, 4, 1: 49–60.

Chappell, C., Rhodes, C., Solomon, N., Tennant, M. and Yates, L. (2003) *Reconstructing the Lifelong Learner: Pedagogy and Identity in Individual, Organisational and Social Change*. London: RoutledgeFalmer.

Charon, J. (2001) *Symbolic Interactionism: An Introduction, an Interpretation, an Integration*. Seventh Edition. Upper Saddle River, NJ: Prentice Hall.

Christie, H., Munroe, M. and Wager, F. (2005) 'Day students' in higher education: widening access students and successful transitions to university life. *International Studies in the Sociology of Education*, 15, 1: 3–30.

Clark, M. (2006) A case study in the acceptance of a new discipline. *Studies in Higher Education*, 31, 2: 133–48.

Clark, R. and Ivanič, R. (1997) *The Politics of Writing*. London: Routledge.

Clegg, S. (2008a) Femininities/masculinities and a sense of self: thinking gendered academic identities and the intellectual self. *Gender and Education*, 20, 3: 209–21.

—— (2008b) Academic identities under threat? *British Journal of Educational Research*, 34, 3: 329–45.

Clegg, S. and Bradley, S. (2006) Models of personal development planning: practice and processes. *British Educational Research Journal*, 32, 1: 57–76.

Coate, K. (2006) Imagining women in the curriculum: the transgressive impossibility of women's studies. *Studies in Higher Education*, 31, 4: 407–21.

Cole, M. (1996) *Cultural Psychology: A Once and Future Discipline*. Cambridge, MA: The Belknapp Press of Harvard University.

Coupland, M. and Crawford, K. (2002) Researching complex systems of activity. Paper presented at the European Association for Research into Learning and Instruction, SIG 10, *Current Issues in Phenomenography*, Canberra, Australia. Available online: www.anu.edu.au/cedam/ilearn/symposium/Coupland.doc (last accessed on 1 October 2008).

Crozier, G., Reay, D., Clayton, J., Colliander, L. and Grinstead, J. (2008) Different strokes for different folks: diverse students in diverse institutions – experiences of higher education. *Research Papers in Education*, 23, 2: 167–77.

Dahlgren, A., Hult, H., Dahlgren, L., Segerstad, H. and Johansson, K. (2006) From senior student to novice worker: learning trajectories in political science, psychology, and mechanical engineering. *Studies in Higher Education*, 31: 569–86.

Davidson, D. (1980) *Essays on Actions and Events*. Oxford: Oxford University Press.

Davies, P. and Mangan, J. (2007) Threshold concepts and the integration of understanding in economics. *Studies in Higher Education*, 32: 711–26.

Davydov, V. (1999) The content and unsolved problems of Activity Theory. In Y. Engeström, R. Miettinen and R-L. Punamäki (eds) *Perspectives on Activity Theory*. Cambridge: Cambridge University Press.

Dawson, S. (2006) A study of the relationship between student communication interaction and sense of community. *Internet and Higher Education*, 9: 153–62.

de Zilwa, D. (2007) Organisational culture and values and the adaptation of academic units in Australian universities. *Higher Education*, 54: 557–74.

Deem, R. and Lucas, L. (2007) Research and teaching cultures in two contrasting UK policy locations: academic life in Education departments in five English and Scottish universities. *Higher Education*, 54: 115–33.

Deer, C. (2003) Bourdieu on higher education: the meaning of the growing integration of educational systems and self-reflective practice. *British Journal of Sociology of Education*, 24, 2: 195–207.

Delamont, S. (1983) *Interaction in the Classroom.* Second Edition. London: Methuen.

Delamont, S. and Atkinson, P. (1995) *Fighting Familiarity: Essays on Ethnography and Education.* Cresskill, NJ: Hampton Press.

Denzin, N. (1992) *Symbolic Interactionism and Cultural Studies: The Politics of Interpretation.* Oxford: Blackwell.

Diaz, M. (2001) Subject, power, and pedagogic discourse. In A. Morais, I. Neves, B. Davies and H. Daniels (eds) *Towards a Sociology of Pedagogy: The Contribution of Basil Bernstein to Research.* New York: Peter Lang.

Dibben, N. (2006) The socio-cultural and learning experiences of music students in a British university. *British Journal of Music Education*, 23, 1: 91–116.

Dowling, P. (1998) *The Sociology of Mathematics of Education: Mathematical Myths/Pedagogical Texts.* London: RoutledgeFalmer.

—— (in press) *Sociology as Method: Departures from the Forensics of Culture, Text and Knowledge.* Rotterdam: Sense.

Drew, L. (ed.) (2008) *The Student Experience in Art and Design Higher Education: Drivers for Change.* Cambridge: Jill Rogers Associates.

Duek, J. (2000) Whose group is it anyway? Equity of student discourse in problem-based learning. In D. Evensen and C. Hmelo (eds) *Problem-Based Learning: A Research Perspective on Learning Interactions.* Mahwah, NJ: Lawrence Erlbaum Associates.

Edwards, A. (2005a) Relational agency: learning to be a resourceful practitioner. *International Journal of Educational Research*, 43: 168–82.

—— (2005b) Let's get beyond community and practice: the many meanings of learning by participating. *The Curriculum Journal*, 16, 1: 49–65.

Edwards, R. (2006) A sticky business? Exploring the 'and' in teaching and learning. *Discourse: Studies in the Cultural Politics of Education*, 27, 1: 121–33.

Engeström, Y. (1987) *Learning by Expanding: An Activity–Theoretical Approach to Developmental Research.* Helsinki: Orienta-Konsultit. Available from: http://lchc.ucsd.edu/MCA/Paper/Engestrom/expanding/toc.htm (last accessed on 1 October 2008).

Engeström, Y. (1990) *Learning, Working and Imagining: Twelve Case Studies in Activity Theory.* Helsinki: Oreinta-Konsultit.

—— (1994) Teachers as collaborative thinkers: activity-theoretical study of an innovative teacher team. In I. Carlgren, G. Handal and S.Vaage (eds) *Teachers' Minds and Actions: Research on Teachers' Thinking and Practice.* London: The Falmer Press.

—— (1995) Objects, contradictions and collaboration in medical cognition: an activity-theoretical perspective. *Artificial Intelligence in Medicine*, 7: 395–412.

—— (1996) Developmental studies of work as a testbench of Activity Theory: the case of primary care medical practice. In S. Chaiklin and J. Lave (eds) *Understanding Practice: Perspectives on Activity and Context.* Cambridge: Cambridge University Press.

—— (1999a) Activity Theory and individual and social transformation. In Y. Engeström, R. Miettinen and R-L. Punamäki (eds) *Perspectives on Activity Theory.* Cambridge: Cambridge University Press.

—— (1999b) *Learning by Expanding: Ten Years After*. Introduction to German Edition of *Learning by Expanding*. http://lchc.ucsd.edu/MCA/Paper/Engestrom/expanding/intro.htm (last accessed on 29 September 2008). Originally published as: *Lernen durch Expansion*. Marburg: BdWi-Verlag.

—— (2000) Activity theory as a framework for analyzing and redesigning work. *Ergonomics*, 43, 7: 960–74.

—— (2001) Expansive learning at work: toward an activity theoretical reconceptualisation. *Journal of Education and Work*, 14, 1: 133–56.

Engeström, Y. and Miettinen, R. (1999) Introduction. In Y. Engeström, R. Miettinen and R-L. Punamäki (eds) *Perspectives on Activity Theory*. Cambridge: Cambridge University Press.

Ensor, P. (2004) Contesting discourse in higher education curriculum restructuring in South Africa. *Higher Education*, 48: 339–59.

Entwistle, N. (1987) A model of the teaching–learning process. In J. Richardson, M. Eysenck and D. Warren Piper (eds) *Student Learning: Research in Education and Cognitive Psychology*. Milton Keynes: Society for Research into Higher Education and Open University Press.

—— (1988) *Styles of Learning and Teaching: An Integrated Outline of Educational Psychology for Students, Teachers and Lecturers*. London: David Fulton Publishers.

—— (2005) Learning outcomes and ways of thinking across contrasting disciplines and settings in higher education. *The Curriculum Journal*, 16: 67–82.

—— (2007) Research into student learning and university teaching. In N. Entwistle and P. Tomlinson (eds) *Student Learning and University Teaching*. Leicester: The British Psychological Society.

Entwistle, N. and McCune, V. (2004) The conceptual bases of study strategy inventories. *Educational Psychology Review*, 16, 4: 324–45.

Entwistle, N. and Ramsden, P. (1983) *Understanding Student Learning*. London: Croom Helm.

Entwistle, N., McCune, V. and Hounsell, J. (2003) Investigating ways of enhancing university teaching–learning environments: measuring students' approaches to studying and perceptions of teaching. In E. De Corte, L. Vershaffel, N. Entwistle and J. van Merriënboer (eds) *Powerful Learning Environments: Unravelling Basic Components and Dimensions*. Oxford: Elsevier Science.

Evans, C. (1993) *English People: The Experience of Teaching and Learning in British Universities*. Buckingham: Open University Press.

Fanghanel, J. (2004) Capturing dissonance in university teacher education environments. *Studies in Higher Education*, 29: 576–90.

—— (2006) *Accounting for Academics' Pedagogical Constructs: Re-Balancing Psychologistic and Structuralist Approaches*. Unpublished Doctoral Thesis, Lancaster University.

—— (2007) Local responses to institutional policy: a discursive approach to positioning. *Studies in Higher Education*, 32: 187–205.

Fejes, A., Johansson, K. and Abrandt, M. (2005) Learning to play the seminar game: students' initial encounters with a basic working form in higher education. *Teaching in Higher Education*, 10: 29–40.

Filer, A. and Pollard, A. (2000) *The Social World of Pupil Assessment: Processes and Contexts of Primary Schooling*. London: Continuum.

Flyvbjerg, B. (2001). *Making Social Science Matter: Why Social Inquiry Fails and How It Can Succeed Again*. Translated by S. Sampson. Cambridge: Cambridge University Press.

Forsyth, A. and Furlong, A. (2000) *Socioeconomic Disadvantage and Access to Higher Education*. Bristol: The Policy Press.

—— (2003) *Losing Out? Socioeconomic Disadvantage and Experience in Further and Higher Education.* Bristol: The Policy Press.

Furlong, A. and Cartmel, F. (2005) *Graduates from Disadvantaged Families: Early Labour Market Experiences.* Bristol: The Policy Press.

Gewirtz, S. and Cribb, A. (2003) Recent readings of social reproduction: four fundamental problematics. *International Studies in Sociology of Education,* 13, 3: 243–60.

Gherardi, S., Nicolini, D. and Odella, F. (1998) Towards a social understanding of how people learn in organizations: the notion of situated curriculum. *Management Learning Journal,* 29, 3: 273–97.

Gibbs, G. and Dunbar-Goddett, H. (2007) *The Effects of Programme Assessment Environments on Student Learning.* York: Higher Education Academy. Available from: www.heacademy.ac.uk/assets/York/documents/ourwork/research/gibbs_0506.pdf (last accessed on 29 September 2008).

Gibbs, G., Habeshaw, T. and Yorke, M. (2000) Institutional learning and teaching strategies in English higher education, *Higher Education,* 40: 351–72.

Giddens, A. (1984) *The Constitution of Society: Outline of the Theory of Structuration.* Cambridge: Polity Press.

Goffman, I. (1959) *The Presentation of Self in Everyday Life.* New York: Doubleday, Anchor Books.

—— (1961) *Asylum: Essays on the Social Situations of Mental Patients and Other Inmates.* New York: Doubleday, Anchor Books.

—— (1963) *Stigma: Notes on the Management of Spoiled Identity.* Englewood Cliffs, NJ: Prentice Hall.

—— (1983) The interaction order. *American Sociological Review,* 48, 1: 1–17.

Gorard, S. (2005) Where shall we widen it? Higher education and the age participation rate in Wales. *Higher Education Quarterly,* 59, 1: 3–18.

—— (2008) Who is missing from higher education? *Cambridge Journal of Education,* 38, 3: 421–37.

Gorard, S. with Adnett, N., May, H., Slack, K., Smith, E. and Thomas, L. (2007) *Overcoming the Barriers to Higher Education.* Stoke on Trent: Trentham Books.

Gow, L. and Kember, D. (1993) Conceptions of teaching and their relation to student learning. *British Journal of Educational Psychology,* 31: 93–7.

Gosling, D. (2008) *Educational Development in the United Kingdom: Report for the Heads of Educational Development Group (HEDG).* London: Heads of Educational Development Group. Available from: www.hedg.ac.uk/documents/HEDG_Report_final.pdf (last accessed on 3 October 2008).

Greasley, K. and Ashworth, P. (2007). The phenomenology of 'approach to studying': the university student's studies within the lifeworld. *British Educational Research Journal,* 33, 6: 819–43.

Grenfell, M. and James, D. (2004) Change *in* the field – chang*ing* the field: Bourdieu and the methodological practice of educational research. *British Journal of Sociology of Education,* 25, 4: 507–23.

Gutiérrez, K., Baquedano-López, P. and Tejeda, C. (1999) Rethinking diversity: hybridity and hybrid language practices in the third space. *Mind, Culture, and Activity,* 6: 286–303.

Haggis, T. (2003) Constructing images of ourselves? A critical investigation into 'approaches to learning' research in higher education. *British Educational Research Journal,* 29: 89–104.

—— (2004), Meaning, identity and 'motivation': expanding what matters in understanding learning in higher education? *Studies in Higher Education,* 29: 335–52.

—— (2006) Context, agency and time: looking at learning from the perspective of complexity and dynamic systems theory. Paper presented at ESRC Teaching and Learning Research Programme Thematic Seminar Series: *Contexts, communities, networks; Mobilising learner's resources and relationships in different domains,* University of Stirling, June 2006.

Hakkarainen, P. (1999) Play and motivation. In Y. Engeström, R. Miettinen and R-L. Punamäki (eds) *Perspectives on Activity Theory.* Cambridge: Cambridge University Press.

Hamilton, M. (2001) Privileged literacies: policy, institutional process and the life of the IALS. *Language and Education,* 15: 92–104.

Hammersley, M. (1980) On interactionist empiricism. In P. Woods (ed.) *Pupil Strategies: Explorations in the Sociology of the School.* London: Croom Helm.

—— (1986) Some reflections on the micro-macro problem in the sociology of education. In M. Hammersley (ed.) *Controversies in Classroom Research.* Second Edition. Buckingham: Open University Press.

—— (2005) What can the literature on communities of practice tell us about educational research? Reflections on some recent proposals. *International Journal of Research and Method in Education,* 28: 5–21.

Hanbury, A., Prosser, M. and Rickinson, M. (2008) The differential impact of UK accredited teaching development programmes on academics' approaches to teaching. *Studies in Higher Education,* 33, 4: 469–83.

Hargreaves, D. (1972) *Interpersonal Relations and Education.* London: Routledge and Kegan Paul.

Harris, S. (2005) Rethinking academic identities in neo-liberal times. *Teaching in Higher Education,* 10, 4: 421–33.

Havnes, A. (2004) Examination and learning: an activity–theoretical analysis of the relationship between assessment and educational practice. *Assessment and Evaluation in Higher Education,* 29, 2: 159–76.

Healey, M. (2005) Linking research and teaching exploring disciplinary spaces and the role of inquiry-based learning. In R. Barnett (ed.) *Reshaping the University: New Relationships Between Research, Scholarship and Teaching.* Maidenhead: Society for Research into Higher Education and Open University Press.

Helland, H. (2007) How does social background affect the grades and grade careers of Norwegian economics students? *British Journal of Sociology of Education,* 28, 4: 489–504.

Henkel, M. (2000) *Academic Identities and Policy Change in Higher Education.* London: Jessica Kingsley Publishers.

—— (2005) Academic identity and autonomy in a changing policy environment. *Higher Education,* 49: 155–76.

Hermerschmidt, M. (1999) Foregrounding background in academic learning. In C. Jones, J. Turner and B. Street (eds) *Students Writing in the University.* Amsterdam/Philadelphia: John Benjamins Publishing Company.

Hernandez-Martinez, P., Black, L., Williams, J., Davis, P., Pampaka, M. and Wake, G. (2008) Mathematics students' aspirations for higher education: class, ethnicity, gender and interpretive repertoire styles. *Research Papers in Education,* 23, 2: 153–65.

Hey, V. (2003) Joining the club? Academia and working-class femininities. *Gender and Education,* 15, 3: 319–35.

Hindess, B. (1988) *Choice, Rationality and Social Theory.* London: Unwin Hyman.

—— (1989) *Political Choice and Social Structure: An Analysis of Actors, Interests and Rationality.* Aldershot: Edward Elgar.

Hodgson, V. (1997) Lectures and the experience of relevance. In F. Marton, D. Hounsell and N. Entwistle (eds) *The Experience of Learning: Implications for Teaching and Studying in Higher Education*. Second edition. Edinburgh: Scottish Academic Press (also available at: www.tla.ed.ac.uk/resources/EoL.html).

Hodkinson, P. and Bloomer, M. (2000) Stokingham Sixth Form College: institutional culture and dispositions to learning. *British Journal of Sociology of Education*, 21, 2: 187–202.

Hodkinson, P. and James, D. (2003) Transforming learning cultures in further education. *Journal of Vocational Education and Training*, 55: 389–406.

Hodkinson, P., Biesta, G. and James, D. (2007) Understanding learning cultures. *Educational Review*, 59, 4: 415–27.

——— (2008) Understanding learning culturally: overcoming the dualism between social and individual views of learning. *Vocations and Learning*, 1: 27–47.

Hodson, P. and Thomas, H. (2003) Quality assurance in higher education: fit for the new millennium or simply year 2000 compliant? *Higher Education*, 45: 375–87.

Holland, D., Lachicotte, W., Skinner, D. and Cain, C. (1998) *Identity and Agency in Cultural Worlds*. Cambridge, MA: Havard University Press.

Holstein, J. and Gubrium, J. (2000) *The Self We Live By: Narrative Identity in a Postmodern World*. Oxford: Oxford University Press.

Hounsell, D. and Hounsell, J. (2007) Teaching–learning environments in contemporary mass higher education. In N. Entwistle and P. Tomlinson (eds) *Student Learning and University Teaching*. Leicester: The British Psychological Society.

Houston, M. and Lebeau, Y. (2006) The social mediation of university learning. *The Social and Organisational Mediation of University Learning (SOMUL): Working Paper 3*. York: Higher Education Academy.

Hutchings, M. (2003a) Information, advice and cultural discourses of higher education. In L. Archer, M. Hutchings and A. Ross (eds) *Higher Education and Social Class: Issues of Exclusion and Inclusion*. London: RoutledgeFalmer.

——— (2003b) Financial barriers to participation. In L. Archer, M. Hutchings and A. Ross (eds) *Higher Education and Social Class: Issues of Exclusion and Inclusion*. London: RoutledgeFalmer.

Ivanič, R. (1998) *Writing and Identity: The Discoursal Construction of Identity in Academic Writing*. Amsterdam/Philadelphia: John Benjamins Publishing Company.

James, D. (2000) Making the graduate: perspectives on student experience of assessment in higher education. In A. Filer (ed.) *Assessment: Social Practice and Social Product*. London: RoutledgeFalmer.

James, D. and Biesta, G. with Colley, H., Davies, J., Gleeson, D., Hodkinson, P., Maull, W., Postlethwaite, K. and Wahlberg, M. (2007) *Improving Learning Cultures in Further Education*. London: Routledge.

James, N. (2007) The learning trajectories of 'old-timers': academic identities and communities of practice in higher education. In J. Hughes, N. Jewson and L. Unwin (eds) *Communities of Practice: Critical Perspectives*. London: Routledge.

Jary, D. and Jones, R. (2006) Overview of widening participation policy and practice. In D. Jary and R. Jones (eds) *Perspectives in Widening Participation in the Social Sciences*. Birmingham: Sociology, Anthropology, Politics (C-SAP), The Higher Education Academy Network.

Jawitz, J. (2007) New academics negotiating communities of practice: learning to swim with the big fish. *Teaching in Higher Education*, 12: 185–97.

Jenkins, A. (2004) *A Guide to the Research Evidence on Teaching–Research Relations*. York: Higher Education Academy.

Jones, C., Turner, J. and Street, B. (eds) (1999) *Students Writing in the University*. Amsterdam: John Benjamin's Publishing Company.

Jones, K., McLean, M., Amigoni, D. and Kinsman, M. (2005) Investigating the production of university English in mass higher education: an alternative methodology. *Arts and Humanities in Higher Education*, 4: 247–64.

Jones, R. and Thomas, L. (2005) The 2003 government higher education white paper: a critical assessment of its implications for the access and widening participation agenda. *Journal of Education Policy*, 20, 5: 615–30.

Kaufman, P. and Feldman, K. (2004) Forming identities in college: a sociological approach. *Research in Higher Education*, 45, 5: 463–96.

Kezar, A. (2006) The impact of institutional size on student engagement. *NASPA Journal*, 43, 1: 87–114.

Kezar, A., Glenn, W., Lester, J. and Nakamoto, J. (2008) Examining organizational contextual features that affect implementation of equity initiatives. *The Journal of Higher Education*, 79, 2: 125–59.

Kleiman, P. (2007) *Thinking, Making, Doing, Solving, Dreaming: Conceptions of Creativity in Learning and Teaching in Higher Education.* Unpublished Doctoral Thesis, Lancaster University.

Knight, P. and Saunders, M. (1999) Understanding teachers' professional cultures through interview: a constructivist approach. *Evaluation and Research in Education*, 13: 144–56.

Knight, P. and Trowler, P. (2000) Department-level cultures and the improvement of learning and teaching. *Studies in Higher Education*, 25, 1: 69–83.

Knight, P., Tait, J. and Yorke, M. (2006) The professional learning of teachers in higher education. *Studies in Higher Education*, 31, 3: 319–39.

Koschmann, T., Glenn, P. and Conlee, M. (2000) When is a problem-based tutorial not a tutorial? Analyzing the tutor's role in the emergence of a learning issue. In D. Evensen and C. Hmelo (eds) *Problem-Based Learning: A Research Perspective on Learning.* Philadelphia: Lawrence Erlbaum Associates Ltd.

Lapping, C. (2005) Antagonism and overdetermination: the production of student positions in contrasting undergraduate disciplines and institutions in the United Kingdom. *British Journal of Sociology of Education*, 26, 5: 657–71.

Latour, B. (2005) *Reassembling the Social: An Introduction to Actor-Network Theory.* Oxford: Oxford University Press.

Laurillard, D. (1997). Styles and approaches in problem-solving. In F. Marton, D. Hounsell and N. Entwistle (eds) *The Experience of Learning: Implications for Teaching and Studying in Higher Education.* Second Edition. Edinburgh: Scottish Academic Press (also available at: www.tla.ed.ac.uk/resources/EoL.html).

Lave, J. (1993) The practice of learning. In S. Chaiklin and J. Lave (eds) *Understanding Practice.* Cambridge: Cambridge University Press.

Lave, J. and Wenger, E. (1991) *Situated Learning: Legitimate Peripheral Participation.* Cambridge: Cambridge University Press.

Law, J. (1994) *Organizing Modernity.* Oxford: Blackwell.

—— (2004) *After Method: Mess in Social Science Research.* London: Routledge.

Layder, D. (1997) *Modern Social Theory: Key Debates and New Directions.* London: UCL Press.

Lea, M. (2005) 'Communities of practice' in higher education: useful heuristic or educational model. In D. Barton and K. Tursting (eds) *Beyond Communities of Practice: Language, Power and Social Context.* Cambridge: Cambridge University Press.

Lea, M. and Street, B. (1998) Student writing in higher education: an academic literacies approach. *Studies in Higher Education*, 23: 157–72.

—— (2006) The academic literacies model: theory and applications. *Theory into Practice*, 45, 4: 368–77.

Leadbetter, J. (2004) The role of mediating artefacts in the work of educational psychologists during consultative conversations in schools. *Educational Review*, 56, 2: 133–45.

Leathwood, C. (2006) Gender, equity and the discourse of the independent learner in higher education. *Higher Education*, 52: 611–33.

Leathwood, C. and O'Connell, P. (2003). It's a struggle: the construction of the 'new student' in higher education. *Journal of Educational Policy*, 18, 6: 597–615.

Leont'ev, A. (1978) *Activity, Consciousness and Personality*. Englewood Cliffs, NJ: Prentice-Hall. Available at: www.marxists.org/archive/leontev/works/1978/index.htm (last accessed on 29 September 2008).

Lillis, T. (1999) Whose 'common sense'? Essaysist literacy and the institutional practice of mystery. In C. Jones, J. Turner and B. Street (eds) *Students Writing in the University*. Amsterdam: John Benjamins Publishing Company.

—— (2001) *Student Writing: Access, Regulation and Desire*. London: Routledge.

Lindblom-Ylänne, S., Trigwell, K., Nevgi, A. and Ashwin, P. (2006) How approaches to teaching are affected by discipline and teaching context. *Studies in Higher Education*, 31: 285–98.

López, J. and Scott, J. (2000) *Social Structure*. Buckingham: Open University Press.

Lucas, L. (2006) *The Research Game in Academic Life*. Buckingham: Society for Research into Higher Education and Open University Press.

—— (2007) Research and teaching work in university education departments: fragmentation or integration. *Journal of Further and Higher Education* 31, 1: 17–30.

Lucas, U. and Mladenovic, R. (2007) The potential of threshold concepts: an emerging framework for educational research and practice. *London Review of Education*, 5: 237–48.

Mackie, M. (2006) Identity, gender and curriculum in architectural studies in the University of Plymouth, UK. In J. Satterthwaite, W. Martin and L. Roberts (eds) *Discourse, Resistance, and Identity Formation: Discourse, Power and Resistance Volume 5*. Stoke on Trent: Trentham Books.

Maines, D. (2001) *The Faultline of Consciousness: A View of Interactionism in Sociology*. New York: Aldine de Gruyter.

Malcolm, J. and Zukas, M. (2001) Bridging pedagogic gaps: conceptual discontinuities in higher education. *Teaching in Higher Education*, 6, 1: 33–42.

Mann, S. (2000) The student's experience of reading. *Higher Education*, 39: 297–317.

—— (2001) Alternative perspectives on the student experience: alienation and engagement. *Studies in Higher Education*, 26, 1: 7–20.

—— (2003) Inquiring into a higher education classroom: insights into the different perspective of teacher and students. In C. Rust (ed.) *Improving student learning: Theory and practice – 10 years on*. Oxford: The Oxford Centre for Staff and Learning Development.

—— (2005) Alienation in the learning environment: a failure of community? *Studies in Higher Education*, 30, 1: 43–55.

Marginson, S. (2008) Global field and global imagining: Bourdieu and worldwide higher education. *British Journal of Sociology of Education*, 29, 3: 303–15.

Martin, E. and Balla, M. (1991) Conceptions of teaching and implications for learning. *Research and Development in Higher Education*, 13: 298–304.

Martin, E., Prosser, M., Trigwell, K., Ramsden, P. and Benjamin, J. (2002) What university teachers teach and how they teach it. In N. Hativa and P. Goodyear (eds) *Teaching Thinking, Beliefs, and Knowledge in Higher Education*. Dordrecht: Kluwer Academic Publishers.

Marton, F. (2007) Towards a pedagogical theory of learning. In N. Entwistle and P. Tomlinson (eds) *Student Learning and University Teaching*. Leicester: The British Psychological Society.

Marton, F. and Booth, S. (1997) *Learning and Awareness*. Mawah, NJ: Lawrence Erlbaum Associates.

Marton, F. and Säljö, R. (1997) Approaches to learning. In F. Marton, D. Hounsell and N. Entwistle (eds) *The Experience of Learning: Implications for Teaching and Studying in Higher Education*. Second edition. Edinburgh: Scottish Academic Press (also available at: www.tla.ed.ac.uk/resources/EoL.html).

Marton, F., Dall'Alba, G. and Beaty, E. (1993). Conceptions of learning. *International Journal of Educational Research*, 19: 277–300.

Maton, K. (2000a) Languages of legitimation: the structuring significance for intellectual fields of strategic knowledge claims. *British Journal of Sociology of Education*, 21, 2: 147–67.

—— (2000b) Recovering pedagogic discourse: a Bernsteinian approach to the sociology of educational knowledge. *Linguistics and Education*, 11, 1: 79–98.

—— (2004) The wrong kind of knower: education, expansion and the epistemic device. In J. Muller, B. Davies and A. Morais (eds) *Reading Bernstein, Researching Bernstein*. London: RoutledgeFalmer.

—— (2005) A question of autonomy: Bourdieu's field approach and higher education policy. *Journal of Education Policy*, 20, 6: 687–704.

—— (2006) On knowledge structures and knower structures. In R. Moore, M. Arnot, J. Beck and H. Daniels (eds) *Knowledge, Power and Educational Reform: Applying the Sociology of Basil Bernstein*. London: Routledge.

—— (2007a) Knowledge- knower structures in intellectual and educational fields. In F. Christie and J. Martin (eds) *Language, Knowledge and Pedagogy: Functional Linguistic and Sociological Approaches*. London: Continuum.

—— (2007b) Segmentalism: the problem of knowledge-building in education, work and life. Paper presented at Explorations in Knowledge, Society and Education, July, University of Cambridge.

Maton, K. and Muller, J. (2007) A sociology for the transmission of knowledges. In F. Christie and J. Martin (eds) *Language, Knowledge and Pedagogy: Functional Linguistic and Sociological Approaches*. London: Continuum.

McCall, M. and Becker, H. (1990) Introduction. In H. Becker and M. McCall (eds) *Symbolic Interaction and Cultural Studies*. Chicago: University of Chicago Press.

McCune, V. and Hounsell, D. (2005) The development of students' ways of thinking and practising in three final-year biology courses. *Higher Education*, 49: 255–89.

McDonough, P. (1997) *Choosing Colleges: How Social Class and Schools Structure Opportunity*. New York: State University of New York Press.

McInnis, C., Griffin, P., James, R. and Coates, H. (2001) *Development of the Course Experience Questionnaire (CEQ)*. Canberra: Department of Education, Training and Youth Affairs.

McKeachie, W. (1974) The decline and fall of the laws of learning. *Educational Researcher*, 3, 3: 7–11.

McLean, M. (2006) *Pedagogy and the University: Critical Theory and Practice*. London: Continuum.

Mead, G. H. (1934) *Mind, Self and Society from the Standpoint of a Social Behaviourist*. Chicago: University of Chicago Press.

Metcalf, H. (2003) Increasing inequality in higher education: the role of term-time working. *Oxford Review of Education*, 29, 3: 315–29.

Meyer, J. and Land, R. (2005) Threshold concepts and troublesome knowledge (2): Epistemological considerations and a conceptual framework for teaching and learning. *Higher Education*, 49: 373–88.

Meyer, J. and Vermunt, J. (eds) (2000) Dissonant study orchestration in higher education: manifestation and effects, *European Journal of Psychology of Education*, whole of the special issue, 15.

Mizra, H. (1995) Black women in higher education: defining a space/finding a place. In L. Morley and V. Walsh (eds) *Feminist Academics: Creative Agents for Change*. London: Taylor and Francis.

Mol, A. and Law, J. (2002) Complexities: an introduction. In J. Law and Mol, A. (eds) *Complexities: Social Studies of Knowledge Practices*. Durham, NC: Duke University Press.

Moore, R. (2000) The (re)organisation of knowledge and assessment for a learning society: the constraints on interdisciplinarity. *Studies in Continuing Education*, 22, 2: 183–99.

—— (2003) Policy driven curriculum restructuring: academic identities in transition. In C. Prichard and P. Trowler (eds) *Realizing Qualitative Research in Higher Education*. Aldershot: Ashgate.

Moore, R. (2004) *Education and Society: Issues and Explanations in the Sociology of Education*. Cambridge: Polity Press.

—— (2006) Knowledge structures and intellectual fields: Basil Bernstein and the sociology of knowledge. In R. Moore, M. Arnot, J. Beck and H. Daniels (eds) *Knowledge, Power and Educational Reform: Applying the Sociology of Basil Bernstein*. London: Routledge.

Moore, R. and Muller, J. (1999) The discourse of 'voice' and the problem of knowledge and identity in the sociology of education. *British Journal of Sociology of Education*, 20, 2: 189–206.

Morrison, K. (2002) *School Leadership and Complexity Theory*. London: RoutledgeFalmer.

Moreau, M-P. and Leathwood, C. (2006) Balancing paid work and studies: working (-class) students in higher education. *Studies in Higher Education*, 31, 1: 23–42.

Mouzelis, N. (1995) *Sociological Theory: What Went Wrong? Diagnosis and Remedies*. London: Routledge.

—— (2000) The subjectivist–objectivist divide: against transcendence. *Sociology*, 34: 741–62.

Muller, J. (2006) On the shoulders of giants: verticality of knowledge and the school curriculum. In R. Moore, M. Arnot, J. Beck and H. Daniels (eds) *Knowledge, Power and Educational Reform: Applying the Sociology of Basil Bernstein*. London: Routledge.

—— (2007) On splitting hairs: hierarchy, knowledge and the school curriculum. In F. Christie and J. Martin (eds) *Language, Knowledge and Pedagogy: Functional Linguistic and Sociological Approaches*. London: Continuum.

Mutch. A. (2003) Communities of practice and habitus: a critique. *Organization Studies*, 24: 383-401.

Mwanza, D. and Engeström, Y. (2005) Managing content in e-learning environments. *British Journal of Educational Technology*, 36, 3: 453–63.

Naidoo, R. (2004) Fields and institutional strategy: Bourdieu on the relationship between higher education, inequality and society. *British Journal of Sociology of Education*, 25, 4: 457–71.

Naidoo, R. and Jamieson, I. (2006) Empowering participants or corroding learning? Towards a research agenda on the impact of student consumerism in higher education. *Journal of Education Policy*, 20, 3: 267–81

Nelson Laird, T., Shoup, R., Kuh, G. and Schwarz, M. (2008) The effects of discipline on deep approaches to student learning and college outcomes. *Research in Higher Education*, 49: 469–94.

Nespor, J. (1994) *Knowledge in Motion: Space, Time and Curriculum in Undergraduate Physics and Management*. London: RoutledgeFalmer.

—— (2007) Curriculum charts and time in undergraduate education. *British Journal of Sociology of Education*, 28, 6: 753–66.

Neumann, R. (2001) Disciplinary differences and university teaching. *Studies in Higher Education*, 26: 135–46.

Neumann, R., Parry, S. and Becher, T. (2002) Teaching and learning in their disciplinary contexts: a conceptual analysis. *Studies in Higher Education*, 27: 405–17.

O'Connor, S. (2008) *A Bernsteinian Analysis of Nursing's Pedagogic Discourse.* Unpublished Doctoral Thesis, Lancaster University.

O'Donnell, V. and Tobbell, J. (2007) The transition of adult students to higher education: legitimate peripheral participation in a community of practice? *Adult Education Quarterly*, 57, 4: 312–28.

O'Donovan, B., Price, M. and Rust, C. (2004) Know what I mean? Enhancing student understanding of assessment standards and criteria. *Teaching in Higher Education*, 9, 3: 325–36.

Olesen, V. and Whittaker, E. (1968) *The Silent Dialogue.* San Francisco: Jossey-Bass.

Ollin, R. (2008) Observing the unobservable: silent pedagogy and teacher/learner positioning in the cultural world of the classroom. Paper presented at British Educational Research Conference, Herriot-Watt University, Edinburgh, 4–6 September 2008.

Ostrove, J. and Long, S. (2007) Social class and belonging: implications for college adjustment. *The Review of Higher Education*, 30, 4: 363–89.

Parker, J. (2002) A new disciplinarity: communities of knowledge, learning and practice. *Teaching in Higher Education*, 7, 4: 373–86.

Parry, G. (2006) Policy-participation trajectories in English higher education. *Higher Education Quarterly*, 60, 4: 392–412.

Paxton, M. (2003) Developing academic literacies in economics in a South African university. *Literacy and Numeracy Studies*, 13, 1: 1–14.

Perkins, D. (2007) Theories of difficulty. In N. Entwistle and P. Tomlinson (eds) *Student Learning and University Teaching.* Leicester: The British Psychological Society.

Pickering, A. (2006) Learning about university teaching: reflections on a research study investigating influences for change. *Teaching in Higher Education*, 11, 3: 319–35.

Pintrich, P. (2004) A conceptual framework for assessing motivation and self-regulated learning in college students. *Educational Psychology Review*, 16, 4: 385–407.

Pollard, A. (1982) A model of classroom coping strategies. *British Journal of Sociology of Education*, 3: 19–37.

—— (1985) *The Social World of the Primary School.* London: Cassell Education.

—— (2007) The Identity and Learning Programme: 'principled pragmatism' in a 12-year longitudinal ethnography. *Ethnography and Education*, 2, 1: 1–19.

Pollard, A. with Filer, A. (1996) *The Social World of Children's Learning: Case Studies of Pupils from Four to Seven.* London: Continuum.

Pollard, A. and Filer, A. (1999a) *The Social World of Pupil Career: Strategic Biographies through Primary School.* London: Continuum.

—— (1999b) Learning, policy and pupil career: issues from a longitudinal ethnography. In M. Hammersley (ed.) *Researching School Experience: Ethnographic Studies of Teaching and Learning.* London: Falmer Press.

—— (2007) Learning, differentiation and strategic action in secondary education: analyses from the Identity and Learning Programme. *British Journal of Sociology of Education*, 28, 4: 441–58.

Power, S., Edwards, T., Whitty, G. and Wigfall, V. (2003) *Education and the Middle Class.* Buckingham: Open University Press.

Price, M. (2005) Assessment standards: the role of communities of practice and the scholarship of assessment. *Assessment and Evaluation in Higher Education*, 3: 215–30.

Price, M., O'Donovan, B., and Rust, C. (2007) Putting a social-constructivist assessment process model into practice: building the feedback loop into the assessment process through peer review. *Innovations in Education and Teaching International*, 44: 143–52.

Prosser, M. and Trigwell, K. (1997) Relations between perceptions of the teaching and environment and approaches to teaching. *British Journal of Educational Psychology*, 67: 25–35.

—— (1999) *Understanding Learning and Teaching: The Experience in Higher Education*. Buckingham: Society for Research into Higher Education and Open University Press.

Prosser, M., Ramsden, P., Trigwell, K. and Martin, E. (2003) Dissonance in experience of teaching and its relation to the quality of student learning. *Studies in Higher Education*, 28: 37–48.

Prosser, M., Martin, E. and Trigwell, K. (2007) Academics' experiences of teaching and of their subject matter understanding. In N. Entwistle and P. Tomlinson (eds) *Student Learning and University Teaching*. Leicester: The British Psychological Society.

Quinn, J. (2004) Understanding working-class 'drop-out' from higher education through a socio-cultural lens: cultural narratives and local contexts. *International Studies in Sociology of Education*, 14, 1: 57–74.

Ramsden, P. (1991) A performance indicator of teaching quality in higher education: The Course Experience Questionnaire. *Studies in Higher Education*, 16, 2: 129–50.

—— (2003) *Learning to Teach in Higher Education*. Second Edition. London: Routledge-Falmer.

Ramsden, P., Prosser, M., Trigwell, K. and Martin, E. (2007) University teachers' experiences of academic leadership and their approaches to teaching. *Learning and Instruction*, 17: 140–55.

Rassool, N. (1995) Black women as 'other' in the academy. In L. Morley and V. Walsh (eds) *Feminist Academics: Creative Agents for Change*. London: Taylor and Francis.

Read, B., Archer, L. and Leathwood, C. (2003) Challenging cultures? Student conceptions of 'belonging' and 'isolation' at a post-1992 university. *Studies in Higher Education*, 28, 3: 261–77.

Reay, D. (1998) 'Always knowing' and 'never being sure': familial and institutional habituses and higher education. *Journal of Education Policy*, 13, 4: 519–29.

—— (2000) 'Dim Dross': marginalised women both inside and outside the academy. *Women's Studies International Forum*, 23, 1: 13–21.

—— (2003) A risky business? Mature working-class women students and access to higher education. *Gender and Education*, 15, 3: 301–17.

—— (2004) 'It's all becoming a habitus': beyond the habitual use of habitus in educational research. *British Journal of Sociology of Education*, 25, 4: 431–44.

Reay, D., David, M. and Ball, S. (2005) *Degrees of Choice: Social Class, Race and Gender in Higher Education*. Stoke on Trent: Trentham Books.

Reay, D., Davies, J., David, M. and Ball, S. (2001) Choices of degree or degrees of choice? Class, 'race', and the higher education choice process. *Sociology*, 35, 4: 855–74.

Reeve, F., Gallacher, J., and Ingram, R. (2007) A comparative study of work-based learning within Higher Nationals in Scotland and Foundation Degrees in England: contrast, complexity, continuity. *Journal of Education and Work*, 20, 4: 305–18.

Richardson, J. (2000) *Researching Student Learning: Approaches to Studying in Campus-based and Distance Education*. Buckingham: Society for Research into Higher Education and Open University Press.

—— (2005) Students' approaches to learning and teachers' approaches to teaching in higher education. *Educational Psychology*, 25: 673–80.

—— (2008) The attainment of ethnic minority students in UK higher education. *Studies in Higher Education*, 33, 1: 33–48.

Richardson, J. and Edmunds, R. (2007) A cognitive-developmental model of university learning. *The Social and Organisational Mediation of University Learning (SOMUL): Working Paper 4*. York: Higher Education Academy.

Richardson, J., Slater, J. and Wilson, J. (2007) The National Student Survey: development, findings and implications. *Studies in Higher Education*, 32, 5: 557–80.

Robbins, D. (1993) The practical importance of Bourdieu's analyses of higher education. *Studies in Higher Education*, 18: 151–64.

Russell, D. (2002) Looking beyond the interface: Activity theory and distributed learning. In M. Lea and K. Nicoll (eds) *Distributed Learning: Social and Cultural Approaches to Learning*. London: RoutledgeFalmer.

Russell, D. and Yañez, A. (2002) 'Big picture people rarely become historians': genre systems and the contradictions of general education. In C. Bazerman and D. Russell (eds) *Writing Selves/Writing Societies: Research from Activity Perspectives*. Fort Collins, CO: The WAC Clearinghouse and Mind, Culture, and Activity. Available at http://wac.colostate.edu/books/selves_societies/ (last accessed on 1 October 2008).

Salomon G. (ed.) (1993) *Distributed Cognitions: Psychological and Educational Considerations*. Cambridge: Cambridge University Press.

Samuelowicz, K. and Bain, J. (1992). Conceptions of teaching held by academic teachers. *Higher Education*, 24: 93–112.

Saunders, M. (2006) From 'organisms' to 'boundaries': the uneven development of theory narratives in education, learning and work connections. *Journal of Education and Work*, 19: 1–27.

Sayer, A. (1992) *Method in Social Science: A Realist Approach*. Second edition, London: Routledge.

—— (2000) *Realism and Social Science*. London: Sage Publications.

Scanlon, E. and Isroff, K. (2005) Activity Theory and higher education: evaluating learning technologies. *Journal of Computer Assisted Learning*, 21: 430–9.

Scott, D. (2000) *Realism and Educational Research: New Perspectives and Possibilities*. London: RoutledgeFalmer.

Scribner, S. and Cole, M. (1981) *The Psychology of Literacy*. Cambridge, MA: Havard University Press.

Severiens, S. and Wolff, R. (2008) A comparison of ethnic minority and majority students: social and academic integration, and quality of learning. *Studies in Higher Education*, 33, 3: 253–66.

Sfard, A. and Prusak, A. (2004) Telling identities: in search of an analytic tool for investigating learning as a culturally shaped activity. *Educational Researcher*, 34, 4: 14–22.

Shay, S. (2004) The assessment of complex performance: a socially-situated interpretive act. *Harvard Educational Review*, 74, 3: 307–329.

—— (2005) The assessment of complex tasks: a double reading. *Studies in Higher Education*, 30, 6: 663–79.

—— (2008) Beyond social constructivist approaches on assessment: the centring of knowledge. *Teaching in Higher Education*, 13, 5: 595–605.

Shreeve, A. (2007) Learning development and study support: an embedded approach through communities of practice. *Art, Design and Communication in Higher Education*, 6: 11–26.

Shreeve, A. (2008) *Transitions: Variation in Tutors' Experience of Practice and Teaching Relations in Art and Design*. Unpublished Doctoral Thesis, Lancaster University.

Sibeon, R. (2004) *Rethinking Social Theory*. London: Sage Publications.

Sikes, P. (2006) Working in a 'new' university: in the shadow of the Research Assessment Exercise? *Studies in Higher Education*, 31, 5: 555–68.

Silverman, D. (2006) *Interpreting Qualitative Data*. Third edition. London: Sage Publications.

Sinfield, S., Burns, T. and Holley, D. (2004) Outsiders looking in or insiders looking out? Widening participation in a post-1992 university. In J. Satterthwaite, E. Atkinson and W. Martin (eds) *The Disciplining of Education: New Languages of Power and Resistance*. Stoke on Trent: Trentham Books.

Singh, P. (2002) Pedagogising knowledge: Bernstein's theory of the pedagogic device. *British Journal of Sociology of Education*, 23, 4: 571–82.

Smith, R. (2007) An overview of research on student support: helping students to achieve or achieving institutional targets? Nurture or de-nature? *Teaching in Higher Education*, 12, 5–6: 683–95.

Solomon, Y. (2007) Not belonging? What makes a functional learner identity in undergraduate mathematics? *Studies in Higher Education*, 32: 79–96.

Strathern, M. (2002) On space and depth. In J. Law and A. Mol (eds) *Complexities: Social Studies of Knowledge Practices*. Durham, NC: Duke University Press.

Strauss, A. (1969) *Mirrors and Masks: The Search for Identity*. Mill Valley, CA: The Sociology Press.

Street, B. (1984) *Literacy in Theory and Practice*. Cambridge: Cambridge University Press.

Tahir, T. (2007) V-Cs attack tax-cut lobbies 'Mickey Mouse' criticisms. *Times Higher Educational Supplement*, 24 August 2007, p. 2.

Taylor, P. (2008) Being an academic today. In R. Barnett and R. Di Napoli (eds) (2008) *Changing Identities in Higher Education: Voicing Perspectives*. London: Routledge.

Teichler, U. (2008) Diversification? Trends and explanations of the shape and size of higher education. *Higher Education*, 56: 349–79.

Thomas, K. (1990) *Gender and the Subject in Higher Education*. Buckingham: Society for Research into Higher Education and Open University Press.

Thomas, L. (2002) Student retention in higher education: the role of institutional habitus. *Journal of Education Policy*, 17, 4: 423–42.

Thomas, L. and Quinn, J. (2007) *First Generation Entry into Higher Education: An International Study*. Maidenhead: Society for Research into Higher Education and Open University Press.

Thurgate, C. and MacGregor, J. (2008) Collaboration in Foundation Degree provision: a case study in Kent. *Journal of Further and Higher Education*, 32, 1: 27–35.

Tierney, W. (1988) Organizational culture in higher education: defining the essentials. *The Journal of Higher Education*, 59, 1: 2–21.

Tight, M. (2003) *Researching Higher Education*. Buckingham: Society for Research into Higher Education and Open University Press.

—— (2004) Research into higher education: an a-theoretical community practice? *Higher Education Research and Development*, 23, 4: 395–411.

—— (2008) Higher education research as tribe, territory and/or community: a co-citation analysis. *Higher Education*, 55: 593–608.

Trigwell, K. (2006) Phenomenography: an approach to research into geography education. *Journal of Geography in Higher Education*, 30, 2: 367–72.

Trigwell, K. and Prosser, M. (1996) Changing approaches to teaching: a relational perspective. *Studies in Higher Education*, 21: 275–84.

Trigwell, K. and Shale, S. (2004) Student learning and the scholarship of university teaching. *Studies in Higher Education,* 29, 4: 523–36.

Trigwell, K., Prosser, M. and Waterhouse, F. (1999). Relations between teachers' approaches to teaching and students' approaches to learning. *Higher Education,* 37: 55–70.

Trowler, P. (1998) *Academics Responding to Change: New Higher Education Frameworks and Academic Cultures.* Buckingham: Society for Research into Higher Education and Open University Press.

—— (2005) A sociology of teaching, learning and enhancement: improving practices in higher education. *Revista de Sociologia,* 76: 13–32.

—— (2008a) *Cultures and Change in Higher Education: Theories and Practice.* Basingstoke: Palgrave Macmillan.

—— (2008b) Beyond epistemological essentialism: academic tribes in the 21st century. In C. Kreber (ed.) *The University and its Disciplines: Teaching and Learning in Higher Education Within and Beyond Disciplinary Boundaries.* London: Routledge.

Trowler, P. and Cooper, A. (2002). Teaching and learning regimes: implicit theories and recurrent practices in the enhancement of teaching and learning through educational development programmes. *Higher Education Research and Development,* 21: 221–40.

Trowler, P. and Knight, P. (1999) Organizational socialization and induction in universities: reconceptualising theory and practice. *Higher Education,* 37: 177–95.

—— (2000) Coming to know in higher education: theorising faculty entry into new work contexts. *Higher Education Research and Development,* 20: 27–42.

Trowler, P. and Wareham, T. (2007) Tribes, territories, research and teaching: enhancing the 'teaching-research nexus'. *Literature Review.* Available at: www.lancs. ac.uk/fass/projects/nexus/outputs.htm (last accessed on 6 October 2008).

Trowler, P., Fanghanel, J. and Wareham, T. (2005) Freeing the chi of change: the Higher Education Academy and enhancing teaching and learning in higher education. *Studies in Higher Education,* 30: 427–44.

Tumen, S., Shulruf, B. and Hattie, J. (2008) Student pathways at the university: patterns and predictors of completion. *Studies in Higher Education,* 33, 3: 233–52.

Tummons, J. (2008) Assessment, and the literacy practices of trainee PCET teachers. *International Journal of Educational Research,* 47, 3: 184–91.

Välimaa, J. (1998) Culture and identity in higher education research. *Higher Education,* 36: 119–38.

Vermunt, J. (2007) The power of teaching–learning environments to influence student learning. In N. Entwistle and P. Tomlinson (eds) *Student Learning and University Teaching.* Leicester: The British Psychological Society.

Vermunt, J. and Verloop, N. (1999) Congruence and friction between learning and teaching. *Learning and Instruction,* 9: 257–80.

Vygotsky, L. (1978) *Mind in Society: The Development of Higher Psychological Processes.* Edited by M. Cole, V. John Steiner, S. Scribner and E. Souberman. Cambridge, MA: Havard University Press.

—— (1986) *Thought and Language.* Edited by A. Kozulin. Cambridge, MA: The Massachusetts Institute of Technology Press.

Warin, J. and Dempster, S. (2007) The salience of gender during the transition to higher education: male students' accounts of performed and authentic identities. *British Educational Research Journal,* 33, 6: 887–903.

Webb, G. (1997) Deconstructing deep and surface: towards a critique of phenomenography. *Higher Education,* 33: 195–12.

Wenger, E. (1998) *Communities of Practice: Learning, Meaning and Identity.* Cambridge: Cambridge University Press.

—— (2000) Communities of practice and social learning systems. *Organization,* 7: 225–46.

Williams, R. (2000) *Making Identity Matter: Identity, Society and Social Interaction.* Durham: Sociology Press.

Wilson, J., Blewitt, J. and Moody, D. (2005) Reconfiguring higher education: the case of foundation degrees. *Education and Training,* 47, 2/3: 112–23.

Windberg, C. (2008) Teaching engineering/engineering teaching: interdisciplinary collaboration and the construction of academic identities. *Teaching in Higher Education,* 13, 3: 353–67.

Woods, P. (1980a) Strategies in teaching and learning. In P. Woods (ed.) *Teacher Strategies: Explorations in the Sociology of the School.* London: Croom Helm.

—— (1980b) The development of pupil strategies. In P. Woods (ed.) *Pupil Strategies: Explorations in the Sociology of the School.* London: Croom Helm.

—— (1983) *Sociology and the School: An Interactionist Viewpoint.* London: Routledge and Kegan Paul.

—— (1996) *Researching the Art of Teaching: Ethnography for Educational Use.* London: Routledge.

Yamagata-Lynch, L. (2003) Using Activity Theory as an analytic lens for examining technology professional development in schools. *Mind, Culture, and Activity,* 10, 2: 100–19.

Yorke, M. (2004) Institutional research and its relevance to the performance of higher education institutions. *Journal of Higher Education Policy and Management,* 26, 2: 141–52.

Yorke, M. and Longden, B. (2007) *The First-Year Experience in Higher Education in the UK: Report on Phase I of a Project Funded by the Higher Education Academy.* York: Higher Education Academy.

Young, M. (2008) *Bringing Knowledge Back In: From Social Constructivism to Social Realism in the Sociology of Education.* London: Routledge.

Zipin, L. (1999) Simplistic fictions in Australian higher education policy debates: a Bourdieuan analysis of complex power struggles. *Discourse: Studies in the Cultural Politics of Education,* 20, 1: 21–39.

Index

Lightning Source UK Ltd.
Milton Keynes UK
25 February 2010

150606UK00001B/26/P